LIFE, ALTERED NOT OVER!

My Silent Journey to Wholeness

Debra D. Winans

Life, Altered Not Over! My Silent Journey to Wholeness

Library of Congress Catalog Information:
ISBN No. 978-1-953443-00-7

Published in Nashville, Tennessee by Durik Advertising

Editor:	Denise Marcia, essentials! the personal development company, Nashville, Tennessee
Copy Edit:	Muriel Puryear, Nashville, Tennessee
Copy Edit:	Dr. Helena Barrington, Talahassee, Florida
Copy Edit:	Dr. Veronica Yon, Talahassee, Florida
Cover Design:	Veronica Hawbaker of Vee Design; Nashville, Tennessee
Cover Photo:	Michael Gomez of Gomez Photography; Nashville, Tennessee
Hair Stylist :	Tanzy Raglon of Salon Mogulz; Nashville, Tennessee
Make-up:	Anna Marie, Nashville, Tennsesse

ENDORSEMENTS

"Nothing can inspire us more than a human story with which we can all relate; a story that encourages us to believe in our own dreams and to have faith in the promises of a God who sometimes seems far away. Debra Winans, in this work **Life, Altered Not Over!** *takes the courage to let us into the private rooms of her silent journey through many of life's narrow passages, and brings us a reason for hope in our own altered lives. This book is destined to be a source of spiritual inspiration for all who explore the wisdom on each page.*

Dr. Myles E. Munroe
Bahamas Faith Ministries
Nassau Bahamas

"Debra deals with the reality of pain and provides an essential tool for hurting people. Having the privilege of traveling around the world and meeting thousands of people (many times in intimate settings), I have witnessed countless pain and struggles that cannot be alleviated because they do not have a "how-to-get-healed" tool. Debra has provided such a tool, this is a great read. **Life, Altered Not Over!** *is a teaching manual and systematic healing tool."*

Bishop Tudor Bismark
Harare Zimbabwe, Africa
Jabula International Ministries

"Only someone who has experienced a tremendous depth of pain and heartbreak could write in such a powerful and refreshing way. I was captivated as I read about Debra's journey, and how her past pain has turned into her present power. You will be challenged to examine your own heart, forgive, and comfort others with the same comfort you have received. I commend Debra's courage for writing this book!"

Nancy Alcorn
Founder of Mercy Ministries
Nashville, Tennessee

Life, Altered Not Over! *is a must read! You and I will always have alterations on our journey to fulfilling purpose. How you respond to diversion determines whether you arrive at the intended destination of all humanity, the real Promise Land.*

Debra Winans is bold, humble and compassionate enough to allow us to travel inside the aspects of her personal life that is usually off limits to the public. For many in the church, it takes courage to agree to divorce, especially when it involves a famous person. Debra did, and she shares her experience. ***Life, Altered Not Over!*** *is a powerful guide to healing and restoration.*

Deborah Bartlett
President - CEO Network
Partner, Bartlett-McWeeney Communications

"Why do some people succeed no matter what obstacles they encounter, while others succumb and lose sight of their dreams in the midst of their adversity? Everyone should take a look into the relentless dedication of Debra Winans', ***Life, Altered Not Over!*** *and glean insight for their own lives as she scales two mountains to their apexes!"*

Pastors Joseph & Yolanda Morgan
Celebration of Life Church
Hendersonville, Tennessee

"In her premier book ***Life, Altered Not Over!*** *Debra Winans helps us to see how God's love and plans for us do not change just because we go through painful difficulties. This book is a life-giver and an essential aid to those who never thought "this" could happen to them. As you journey through this book soak in every word. Allow Debra's life to coach you, teach you, minister to you, and transform you."*

Lee Jenkins
Nationally recognized
Financial Adviser, Author, and Teacher
Atlanta, Georgia

"Debra Winans is on a journey…just like you and me. Filled with unknown twists and curves she did not plan, her journey is our journey to find authenticity in our lives. This book, ***Life, Altered Not Over!*** *tells her story in a relatable format that will bring freedom to the reader. You will find "all that glitters is not gold," but once tried in the fire, pure gold will emerge."*

Dr. Shirley Arnold
Shirley Arnold Ministries
Lakeland, Florida

"Spirituality accompanied by wisdom and originality is a rare combination in today's contemporary environment. Debra Winans' story – ***Life, Altered Not Over!*** *is certainly a masterpiece in victoriously coming to terms with life's crises and fulfilling God's plan. Her insights are provocative and sincere, with a refreshing approach to facing the challenges of life – she is wise beyond her years.*

I highly recommend this book to all who need to know that God is there in the midst of their darkness. His Word tells us that He will never leave us nor forsake us, and this author brilliantly reinforces that promise, reminding us to draw on His strength, especially when our path is unexpectedly altered. This decidedly credible work is a must read."

Dr. Victoria E. Jones
Dean, College of Leadership
Director of Human Resources
General Motors Corporation

"When you read Debra Winans' book, you must bear in mind that it is the journey beyond. Beyond what? The dilemmas that bind us to our past and hinder us from progressing into our future. Isaiah 54:17 reminds us that "No weapon formed against us will prosper." The word "form" means the enemy has strategically fashioned and tailor-

made a device that is loaded with our hang-ups and weaknesses, along with our spiritual, physical, and yes, emotional DNA coded within, with the express purpose of blocking our journey to success.

Debra's book, **Life, Altered Not Over!** *offers a rare treasure of hope. It will help us to confidently embrace the journey beyond – knowing the best is yet to come!"*

Pastor Beverly Martin, Ph.D.
Dayton, Ohio

"Debra writes with such candid and inspirational insight, sharing personal stories that speak to the importance of listening to the voice of God in all we do, and positioning ourselves to accept change that most times make us uncomfortable. This book will help you to really look within yourself to reflect upon the life experience that has somewhat altered your life...sometimes creating a moment of loneliness, silence, or even pain. But one reality that is made clear in the content of this book... "God will never leave you." He will take that silent journey with you as you transition from one phase of life to the next. Debra, thank you for being so honest and sharing your heart. I know many will be blessed."

Dr. Janice Crenshaw, RN, BSN, MSN
The Studer Group
Gulf Breeze, Florida

"One thing that is missing in the Body of Christ is a sound, biblical understanding of how to handle life's setbacks. Debra allows herself to be transparent enough to teach us that God is sovereign and absolutely in control of whatever life brings our way.

As I began to read this book I cried, laughed, I wiped my tears and even reached through the pages to wipe Debra's also. Then I journeyed further into the book. As I got to the end, my tears were dried, my joy was full and I stood applauding Debra for her victory and the contribution that she has now made to the Body of Christ. If it is true that our theology is shaped by our tragedies, then Debra's struggles have earned her a Th.D. What a wonderful dissertation!"

Bishop Vaughn McLaughlin
Senior Pastor and CEO
Potter's House Church
Jacksonville, Florida

"I remember being asked whether or not anybody would read a book about my life story. My answer...probably not. Debra Winans, however, has compiled pages of life experience that I believe will edify, encourage, and uplift the readers. Most authors that write novels of this nature usually come across bitter and resentful. This book is far from the usual man-bashing, vent fest that wounded people have a tendency of flocking to. I truly believe those that have had "life" happen to them can find healing, help, and restoration in these comforting passages. There is still life in you!"

Jonathan Miller
YPJ (Youth Pastor Jonathan)
Faith Apostolic Church
South Bend, Indiana

"As a former Vice President of Human Resources for National Fortune 500 Companies, the heroine of this book, ***Life, Altered Not Over!****, embodies characteristics that I have been teaching business women for years – poise, confidence, and the realization that setbacks create opportunities for promotions! Debra Winans' resilience, passion, and humor will inspire all women, from household managers to corporate executives."*

Brenda Scott
Owner/Consultant
Integrity Employment Services, LLC

DEDICATION

This book is dedicated to the memories of three of the most influential women in my life: my mother, Myrtle Johnson, who was my greatest influence; my older and only sister, Dianne Johnson, who was most significant in my development; and Rev. Evelyn Spencer, affectionately known as "Rev. Ev," my spiritual mother. She not only saw greatness in me but told me I would not be content doing anything other than what I was created to do and be.

Even though none of these women lived to see the fruit of their labor come to pass in my life, I honor them by committing to complete my journey; by walking in obedience to Almighty God. In memoriam, I say my life isn't over because of what all of you have instilled in me.

ACKNOWLEDGMENTS

Lord Jesus, there aren't enough words in any language that express how much I love You. There were times I could not trace You but I knew I could trust You. I live because of You. Thank You for entrusting me with such an assignment. My whole life belongs to You.

To my children Miya and Benjamin, I'm grateful God trusts me to love, teach and train you. I can't love you enough. You bring so much joy to my life. Thank you for the many hugs, love notes and kisses. You're the reason I do what I do; so I can ensure that the torch is passed on to you. You both are created for greatness. Do what you were created to do with joy and success. Mommy sure believes in you!

To my five brothers: Flynn, Richard, David, Rodney and Steve, who taught me that "real men" love, lead and protect their families. You were my first recollection of genuine protection and leadership. To my sisters-in-law; Carolyn, Veronica, Bonnie, Gayla and Alisha, thank you for the love you share that goes beyond being in-laws but real sisters. I love you.

To my pastors Joseph & Yolanda Morgan, your leadership, wisdom, encouragement and faith in me plays a significant role in my existence. Under your leadership I have grown tremendously and have been healed miraculously. You are indeed shepherds after God's own heart. I love and appreciate you both.

To Bishop Flynn & Carolyn Johnson who raised me after our Mom passed away. Because of your example, I have a passion to serve the Lord today. You taught me how to dream and how to walk through adversity. Love you much.

To my mentor Bishop Judy Anderson, thank you for empowering me to be the woman for the job. Your faith in me has caused me to soar beyond my wildest dreams. You are the bomb!

Drs. Kennith & Helena Barrington, my godparents. To speak of you is a book within itself! Your unwavering love has been constant over twenty-plus years. Your wisdom, patience, listening ear and parenting are what shaped me into the woman I am today. To you I say, thank you.

And to all those who encouraged me throughout the years to finish this book along with the other assignments I've been commissioned to fulfill, I'd like to thank you. Special thank you to: Lynnette Bullock, Veronica Hawbaker, Anderia Stewart, the Miller families in South Bend, and Indianapolis, and many others. You know who you are. I am truly grateful for you all.

PREFACE

"And we know that all things work together for the good to them that love God, to them that are the called according to His purpose." [Romans 8:28, NKJV]

One of the greatest delights of my life has been the God-ordained privilege of knowing Debra D. Winans and accepting the call to participate in her nurture and growth. She has a story to tell, and I am thoroughly elated that she has begun to tell it. I choose to say "she has begun..." because this offering you are now reading is but a preamble to a significant and ongoing journey.

Throughout her formative years, she was provided the first and foremost tool she would need for the journey that her life would take: a solid, Christian foundation, built through an intense labor of love. When my husband and I were chosen to be her godparents, this foundation had already been laid. Our assignment was to provide reinforcement to that foundation and enlarge upon it, sanctioning the "liberty with boundaries" given her by those who had the weightier responsibility; all within the reassuring environment of unconditional love. WOW! What a joy!

We had the easy part! It was not perfect because we're not perfect. However, the strength of character developed within her was so phenomenal that even after an occasional emotional tantrum (although few and far between), she just had a way of making light the hearts of those around her. Debra's constant sense of awe and wonder made her a joy to be with. Thank God that through all her experiences, life has not robbed her of that childlike sense of amazement.

Debra's personal style and wit reveal maturity, a deep compassion for people, an intelligent and perceptive mind, as well as a true servant's heart. She demonstrates a firm grasp on the principles of love and forgiveness that bring healing and restoration. As she shares her heart and her journey, allow the Lord to reveal to you the matters of your heart that can bring you into that "Aha" moment of Divine destiny. Let the journey begin...

Dr. Helena Barrington
Founder, Metropolitan Christian Academy of the Arts
Tallahassee, Florida

FOREWORD

As I reflect on our first meeting years ago, the strong sense of spiritual significance and spiritual ties once again flood my emotions and memory. The Spirit of God had united us in ministry. While kneeling beside Debra, I was made aware of her hidden pain, and the cry of her soul for spiritual direction. In that moment, I saw her need for clarity and spiritual encouragement. Yet, I also knew of her bold faith and her quiet inner strength. Then I heard the Spirit whisper, "Yes with all of her pain, I have called her to be a strong servant-leader and to minister to the brokenness of humanity."

Debra Winans' writings in this book, ***Life, Altered Not Over!*** are not only what I call "strong medicine" for the Body of Christ, but much needed medicine. She presents a wisdom which can only be gained through personal experience. Debra offers each encounter and event with a burst of sincere and authentic passion. Whenever a writer provokes the reader to enter into the spirit and soul of their manuscript – to the extent that the reader experiences every emotion of the writer – it is called "enactment." Enactment allows the reader to transcend the mental and spiritual intent of the writer. Most often we call this a "catharsis."

By the time I had read "Fact Is, Truth Is" I had arrived at my catharsis. When I reached the end of Debra's journey, I found myself re-examining areas of my past experiences and applying what I found to be key prescriptions that Debra provides in this book – forgiveness, love and endurance!

We who have imparted faith and friendship into Debra's life are elated that she has chosen to share this book of her difficult but honest journey with you. You will be blessed and encouraged as she moves you gracefully through the pages, and you discover her growth and new-found wisdom in God. I am confident that this "journal" is just the beginning of her call to minister truth with clarity to the Bride of Christ. Take a deep breath and exhale. You too will be blessed as you travel Debra's fascinating journey to wholeness.

Elaine S. Waller, Ph.D.
Senior Counselor/Director
Transformation Counseling Outreach Center
Virginia Beach, Virginia

CONTENTS

INTRODUCTION

I'm reminded of a line from a movie that said, *"Why are you trying to blend in, when you were born to stand out?"* Those words hit me like a ton of bricks. I could not shake them for months; they touched the very core of my being. That phrase kept resonating like a constant nightmare…it just would not go away. (Think about that statement for a moment.)

So many of us have spent our lives trying to 'blend' into a place for which we were not intended. Hiding not only from what we've been called to do, but who we truly are! We can trace this struggle as far back as our childhood and well into our adult lives, still with the questions remaining, "Who am I and why am I here? Where do I fit? Why and how have I survived so much in my lifetime?"

So, we travel through time trying to find our place in this world of complexity, desperately wanting to make sense out of life along with our constant pursuit of dreams that may or may not come to pass. We also face the drama of broken relationships and heartaches and for most, that seems to be an acceptable way of life. When we take a stroll down life's boardwalk, it leaves us scratching our heads in awe. With furrowed brow we ask the questions: How did I get here? What was I thinking? When will this end? Where did I drop the ball? Why didn't I see that coming? How? What? When? Where? Why? The onslaught of questions seem to have no end, rhyme or reason. Ahh, but there is an end…an unexpected end!

I wrote this book because those were *my* questions, as well as the questions of so many other people I know – male and female. I was on a quest to discover Debra's true identity. I needed to know the light I saw at the end of the tunnel was indeed a light of *hope* and not the light of yet another oncoming train.

I have always been known as the one who would walk with folks through *their crises*, straight to the end. However, at the end of the day, I was all alone. I have often asked myself, 'How can the one, who encourages others to live, now seem to feel so lifeless?' And, 'How is it that the one who so often gives hope, ends up feeling so hopeless?' You may be like me, one who would walk on hot coals for a friend but in the end find yourself sitting in the ashes.

Is it possible we are the channel needed for someone else to just "be" – the conduit through which God can do it? Heal us? Maybe we are the stream life has been designed to flow through? Ironically, we may even function as a syringe, an instrument through which the healing agent flows, yet once the syringe is used, it ends up discarded.

Perhaps like myself, you my friend, could be the antidote, the neutralizer, the antitoxin, the counter-reacting agent, the vaccine that gives life and hope! What a prescription for those who have been hurt in life! You may be the very source of healing for someone you don't even know. So stop blending in and start standing out. Many hurting people are waiting for you!

My hope is that while you are reading this book you will take note of the challenges I have been accosted by in life and discover that you too can overcome the pain, overcome the hurt, the loss of friends, and even the loss of your own identity. Perceive this my friend; your life isn't over after all!

Debra D. Winans

JOURNEY ONE

Too Many Voices

Dreamer of big dreams, that's me! I've had dreams of traveling the world and owning successful businesses. I've had dreams of becoming a philanthropist. I've had dreams of owning property all over the globe. I've had dreams of loving and being in love like in the fairy tale, *Cinderella*. I've even had dreams of flying to the moon! But one thing I *never* dreamt, in my wildest imagination was to go through a legal separation that ended in an unwanted divorce. Devastation raised its ugly head and caused not only monstrous pain but inconceivable confusion.

The highlight of my afternoons and evenings then had been rocking both my three-year-old daughter and my four-month-old son. They would snuggle together on my lap; the sweet smell of innocence and baby breath would temporarily anesthetize me from the madness of my marital issues. The doom of impending division with my spouse left me thinking; life couldn't get any worse than this, could it? My life was shattering. My heart was filled with uncertainty. Me, the Christian woman with strong faith and values who stood before hundreds of people declaring, "You can walk through **any** situation and circumstance V-I-C-T-O-R-I-O-S-L-Y!"

Now, I was being challenged. I became first partaker of my very own words. I thought I could shout victory on the mountain top…and I could. However, I neglected to calculate the depth of the pain I would face and endure. I was not so sure how to walk this road called 'Up Close and Personal.' I had judged others in similar situations and in my opinion, they should have been able to discern and ward off such tragedy. Now having first-hand experience, my judgment quickly turned to conviction that led to heart-felt repentance.

Reluctant and afraid to take steps in any direction, I was paralyzed. Not only that, to simply put one foot in front of the other was like treading in quick sand. Something as natural as breathing now took concentrated effort. I was trying to look capable but God wanted me to lean on Him. He was requiring me to draw upon His strength; and even in my anguish, I was continually reminded His strength is perfect in my weakness.

How do I raise my two babies? What do I tell them? What do I tell myself? Where do I go from here? This cannot be happening! Divorced? Me? My mind was racing so fast I couldn't keep up with my own thoughts.

After putting my babies to bed, I began piddling around the house. I went through each room reminiscing in every place that once represented our whole family. His closet that bulged with designer suits and clothing was now vacant. The chest-of-drawers that stored his color-coordinated socks, belts, underwear, and tee shirts were empty. The aroma of his cologne that once filled our room had now completely dissipated. Every award and plaque that had been neatly and proudly placed on display was now gone leaving only dust and fingerprints behind. Our house, complete with a Baby Grand piano on which his chocolate fingers danced and filled the atmosphere with new music, was now filled with silence. It was too quiet. The babies were asleep; there was no music, no laughter and no masculine presence.

Loneliness, isolation, resentment and uncertainty were the only voices I could hear. I hated the seclusion. I despised the quiet, and I loathed the desertion.

Loneliness, isolation, resentment and uncertainty were the only voices I could hear. I hated the seclusion. I despised the quiet, and I loathed the desertion. I look back now in awe of how far I've come, but not without a price...a costly price. Do you ever wonder why the price to move to the next dimension of emotional development is so incredibly high? Hmmm...

The day of my piddling was also a day of reflecting, examining, pondering, and facing. I came across my old journals of thoughts, questions, and personal examination. It was not customary for me to review what I had previously written, so my reading those pages for the first time was strange yet enlightening. Page after page I saw recurrences of painful and misplaced emotions. I discovered I had been here before, numerous times in fact. They obviously lacked his and my discussion, which unfortunately led to more conflict and finally marital dissolution.

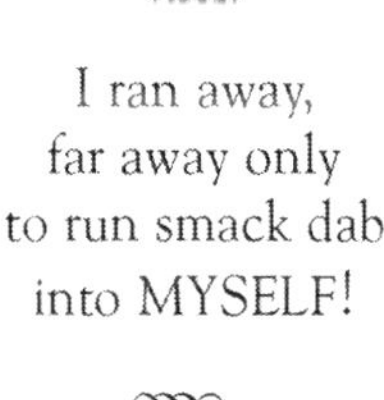

Why weren't these issues addressed? I was screaming at the top of my lungs, why couldn't he hear me? Why didn't he rescue me? You mean that huge sign on my forehead...WIFE HURTING, PLEASE HELP! went completely unnoticed? My journals spoke of the unspoken, the 'better-left-alone' category. I found journaling to be my way of escape. My soliloquy expressed what he refused to hear, my cry, my pain as the wife of his youth. Screams unheard? Yes. Rescued? Not that day. Help needed? Wait – it's coming.

As much as I wanted to play the victim, the time had come to take a hard look in the pool of reflection like Simba in *The Lion King!* As I looked *h-h-h-a-w-d-a,* I didn't run to the Pride Land to rebuild what had been destroyed; I ran away, far away only to run smack dab into MYSELF!

Now please don't misunderstand me, I take responsibility as well. I could have made better choices. I should not have feared the truth by burying my head in the sand. In many instances I held my tongue when I shouldn't have. I tolerated his unhealthy friendships far too long. I failed to be completely honest with issues I brought into the marriage. I learned well to skirt around – better yet, I *hid* behind my issues in work, ministry and even family. I should not have ignored the signs of his impudent behavior. I presumed I could pray it go away with time. Falsely thinking I could handle our marriage in the condition it was in; but then I discovered my own pride, the pride to think I can do it all myself and cover up the embarrassment of a failed high-profile marriage. And what for? Who did I think I was? I was trying to take God's place. My bad, life is to be lived not engaged in constant turmoil.

> *I learned well to skirt around – better yet, I hid behind my issues in work, ministry and even family.*

Since he was the head of our family there were definitely areas in which he could have healed us. Such as, investing in the sanctity of our marriage or giving of himself to our family as much as to his career, spending not *more* time but just *time*, and depositing in our relationship with more than *things* and *gifts*. The occasional, "I'm sorry, I was wrong," and/or "forgive me," would have been more than welcomed. I needed a husband, a friend and a covering. Nonetheless, I'm taking you through a series of events which led to *my* journey to wholeness.

My journals were filled with events of a process with no guidance, reflecting pent-up emotions, which remained on the pages of time. I was in trouble. My self-esteem was shot to an all time low. I was trying to find my place in all the madness, a whirlwind of entertainment, ministry, fans, and family. My marriage was a hot mess! My disintegrating marriage was like a castle built on the sand left to be washed away by the rush of the ocean waves.

I successfully walked with several couples through their marriage issues, the wisdom I gave them worked! In fact, each couple is still together today and doing well, might I add. Surely this will work for me as well, right? So here I go, on the best road anyone and everyone should take in my situation, counseling…so I thought.

I heard so many voices: recommendations, opinions, formulas, doctrines, and so on. Trying to do what's right, I trusted each one who gave me counsel...."For there is safety in the multitude of counselors" (Prov 11:14 NKJV). I desired my marriage to work so much I'd jump through all types of hoops! I was instructed to do this, that, and the other, 'This time it will work,' I thought; it has to. People are watching, expecting, praying, hoping, whispering, pointing, waiting to see what will happen, whether their predictions were correct. With all the pressure I added to my plate, surely I'll be able to place a trophy of marital success from my own life as I shut the mouths of the "naysayers."

> *People are watching, expecting, praying, hoping, whispering, pointing, waiting to see what will happen, whether their predictions were correct.*

"Okay, what should I do next?"

I was told by one well-meaning counselor: *Go through your house, bless and anoint every door post with oil. Rebuke the devil, fast for three days; stay on your face and watch God move. Watch God restore your marriage better than ever.*

Someone else told me: *God will honor the spouse that stays in the home.*

Another counselor said: *God is obligated to move for you Debra so stand on His Word.*

It was also suggested: *You shouldn't file [for divorce] first; the greater judgment would be on you. Stand still.*

Another voice: *Fight Debra, put on something sexy; comb your hair over to your left eye and wait. Make him an offer he can't refuse. You should fly out to meet him, I'm sure he'll be happy to see you!*

And another encouraged me to: *Pray Debra, don't stop praying. Sometimes women have to take more, that's how we're built, to take* ***it****, whatever* ***it*** *is.*

It was a counselor who told me: *More is required of you because of the anointing and call on your life. You've got to suffer. You must humble yourself, take down, come low, admit you were wrong and take the responsibility to bring peace. Read these Scriptures daily, memorize them. You have some issues you need to deal with and until you deal with you consistently, you will always be at this place. Make sure there's nothing in you the enemy can use. Pray girl, P-R-A-Y. You're the strong one. Sow a seed for a restored marriage.*

> Another proclaimed: *You must be broken, we all have to be broken Debra, and so make sure you pass this test.*

An exhaustive litany of advice and wisdom was lovingly given to me. Each person sensed my pain and frustration, all hoping for a 180 degree turn for the betterment of our family.

> *I had forgotten that God is sovereign, people are not.*

I fought. I did not waver. I anointed every door post. I stood on and read the Word of God. I followed the instructions to the best of my ability. I prayed and prayed and prayed and prayed some more. I repented of everything and anything I could think of. I searched and re-searched myself. I wanted to be right before God. Whatever was suggested, I attempted to do it. And as instructed, I did not file first. Obedience was at the forefront of my heart and actions. I believed in those who counseled me, for they are credible people. These are men and women of integrity. I trusted them. I trusted their wisdom. We all wanted the same thing, restoration and wholeness of my marriage.

> *My disintegrating marriage was like a castle built on the sand left to be washed away by the rush of the ocean waves.*

Now, three-and-a-half years had come and gone. My situation was not restored. It did not change for the better. It was not better than ever; as a matter of fact, it was worse. What had been a legal separation has now become a full-blown divorce, reviewed in the local newspaper and a few national magazines as well. Now, who should I blame? No one. Who missed God? No one. I had imagined the TBN, Oprah Winfrey, and Dr. Phil testimony to show how God worked a miracle at 11:59! Yet a restored marriage was not the miracle I would experience. I was not whole, but still very broken and by now, weary.

There was no guarantee that adhering to the specifications and instructions of the godly folk would give me marital success. I had forgotten that God is sovereign, people are not. This was a reality that was challenging for me to face, because submitting to leadership was how I was reared. However, the reality of my situation did not negate the appropriate teachings of the leaders. Authority and headship is ordained by God. But, I found it made me ultimately responsible for the Word and voice of God for *myself and my daily living.*

Instead of the nationally publicized testimony, my miracles were quiet, private, subtle, and low-key with not one single person around to witness them. My miracles were so private it has taken years to share them publicly. This is the journey that forever changed my life. As painful and lengthy as this process was, every scar, betrayal, sin, and acts of forgiveness have developed me into a *better woman*, not a *bitter woman.*

Truly, there is no testimony without the test. No victory without failure. No gain without pain. No rowing forward without the oars moving backwards. Dancers can't leap without a plie'. Cliché yes, but nonetheless, I found each to be a valued truth.

If you intricately trace the life of someone you believe to be successful, what you detect is not only the applause of men for a job well done, but the hindrances within that person, such as insecurities, failures, and resentments. We all have issues. We are all guilty of listening to someone else's voice, whether friend, foe, or even our own. The challenge is in the midst of all we hear; we must find a way to decipher the importance of what is said, and to discern *if, when and how we are to follow.*

Counseling can be beneficial. But to reap its full benefits, all parties involved must be prepared to be honest and forthright. It is the only way to bring <u>any</u> resolution. And understand this: Healing almost without exception is accomplished through pain. As for me, this was a frightening experience, being uncovered and naked without any healing ointment applied to my deep-seated emotional wounds; it left me feeling completely exposed. Unfortunately, I was guilty of being too busy trying to conceal what I didn't want unmasked in order to bring peace, which wasn't peace at all, just the delay of the inevitable – a terminated marriage.

Counseling is only as effective as the truth and openness you are willing to reveal. If your intention is to conceal the other person or yourself, you cannot expect total healing or any truthful results. You are not covering; you are actually enabling the person to remain the same and prolong his or her need, as well as your own, to be made whole.

The process of self-examination is an individual designated walk. No rescue mission for this girl. No quick fix. No microwave results today! The bottom line is this, not one single person could fix my problems, only me and the Lord. Your journey begins and ends with the Lord <u>and</u> you.

Maturity is required in order for a person to acknowledge he or she has seriously blown it. It takes a mature person to admit he or she doesn't have the answers and their way of solving matters has not worked, but has come to grips recognizing that considerable help is needed. Pointing fingers is a waste of time when in many cases, the one pointing is often-times the most guilty. The sobering aspect is Rome was not built in a day. Neither was your situation. Be patient with yourself. It takes time to walk through any process of life.

In a sincere effort to not be too graphic, I want to disclose a few short statements of pain I've been given permission by others to repeat. Maybe you've been here, said this, done that...

"You don't have a clue what I've been through, they hurt me beyond repair – I was devastated." ~ *"You don't know what they did to destroy our family. I almost lost my mind!"* ~ *"I'm on five different medications just to function as a result of what happened to me."* ~ *"Man, she destroyed my dreams and my business and she made me feel less than a man."* ~ *"I was loyal, I was there. Tell you what, I will* ***never*** *trust again."* ~ *"She turned my children against me. Now what will they think of me? How will they ever know the real truth?"* ~ *"I covered and protected. I could have been vindictive, but instead I needed to protect the children. It's the right thing to do, right?"* ~ *"I can better handle him leaving me for a woman, but I can't understand him leaving me for a man."* ~ *"I should have seen this coming, I thought I had enough strength and love for the both of us. Maybe love*

isn't enough after all." ~ *"The emotional scars are more damaging than the physically inflicted ones. No one would ever believe he beats me on the regular, and then stands in the pulpit every Sunday."* ~ *"I'm married to a public figure. I can't believe I've become the very thing I despised. Who will believe me? He has too much influence and power."* ~ *"I kept all his secrets but he exposed mine."* ~ *"He lied to the judge and my children were temporarily taken from me. He didn't want to raise them. It was all about* ***his*** *image."* ~ *"Oh God, help me please. No one would ever believe me if I told this..."*

More often than not, you chose to be silent rather than make a public spectacle of yourself and the situation. These are real statements. It's what I call the uncensored version. You may have heard worse, or perhaps your story is deeper and more intricate. Even though these tell-all statements are hurtful and true, what I'm after more so are the thought-provoking questions they raise.

As much as life isn't fair and it may or may not have been your fault, the real questions remain. Now that you are here in "this place," what is the purpose of your survival? Why isn't life over? You survived that and even that? Justified as you felt you were, you still didn't destroy anyone. Did you? You have asked yourself, *"What in the world am I supposed to do with all this pain? Counseling doesn't seem to give me the results I expected."*

If the formulas or counsel you may have been given didn't work, what attitude will you develop? Who's to take responsibility for the outcome? Let's take it up a notch: Will you despise and blame God for allowing such tragedies to occur?

Voices have the ability to carry great weight along with great responsibility. As I stated earlier in this chapter, those who gave me counsel shared what they felt was correct and Godly. However, sometimes it's easier or, better said, convenient to simply **take** the advice, wisdom, or counsel of another when you not only are in dire straits, but also are dealing with situations which are unseemly and explosive in your own mind.

What a challenge it is to focus, to hear, or to see when your own residence and mind <u>is</u> the battlefield! All you know is what you've tried is not working and has not worked for some time now. *The pressure, Oh! The pressure, I need some relief…!* But relief denotes a quick deliverance when going through the process which is tedious and essentially necessary. The counsel and wisdom of others can cause a dependency which, in reality can keep you from taking some responsibility for where you are, how you got there and how you pursue its resolution. The process of teaching and instructing others takes time, energy and patience. The quick and simple solution (which isn't a solution at all) is to do the job for your children, employees, members, or counselees and family, rather than to take the time to teach, and instruct them or walk them through it.

> *"What in the world am I supposed to do with all this pain? Counseling doesn't seem to give me the results I expected."*

For example, I wanted and believed someone should've given me the answers to my dilemma; after all I was the one in counseling. I was the one seeking the truth. I was the one fighting for the family. I wanted, needed, and deserved answers...NOW! RIGHT NOW! After all my standing, praying and waiting; somebody better answer me quickly! *You're a pastor, fix this! You're a professional counselor, fix this! Shouldn't you rebuke him for his actions? You've heard this before, fix this! That's your job to fix things! Now fix THIS!* But the truth of the matter is, this was my cry of desperation and I wasn't willing to allow desperation to lead me through the process of wholeness. Counseling did not save my marriage. But the epiphany revealed through counseling saved me. Saving me is what my life's journey was about; it's the screenplay for the coming attraction!

I discovered pressure will blow your cover. You will discover what you are authentically made of. You can tow the line all you like but pressure allows you the opportunity to examine yourself h-h-h-a-w-d-a! In every dark place, eventually a purpose is revealed. My pastor says it like this, "*When going through hell, do not stop, keep moving. There is a purpose in it all; go through it until that purpose is revealed."* See, my purpose and your purpose is accomplished in our process.

> *"When going through hell, do not stop, keep moving. There is a purpose in it all; go through it until that purpose is revealed."*

The most lethal weapon in my arsenal was what I took back from the enemy of my soul and turned on him. I didn't know I was a warrior until I journeyed to a place called ***Still*** – the place where much soul-searching, fighting through and listening intently took on a new meaning and where life began to make some sense. I needed insight into what I was going through.

So, before you move forward, let's step backward to a place called ***The Beginning***. But first pray this ample prayer with me:

"God grant me the serenity to accept the people I cannot change, the courage to change the one I can, and the wisdom to know…it's me!"

(John B. Miller author of *QBQ-Question Behind the Question*)

Consider your journey and write your story.

Some journey, yes? Keep writing.

JOURNEY TWO

In the Beginning Was a Baby Girl

It's a GIRL!" My father said at my birth. The fulfillment of longing hearts was finally realized. First there was the oldest child Dianne, then five 'hard-headed' boys came in a row, and now finally another girl joined the Johnson clan. "She's here! I can't believe she's finally here!" my mother cried tears of joy. Baby girl, Debra Denise was born out of an intense marital love affair, shared through the legacy that would come.

My brother Richard told me wonderful stories of the love my parents, Walter and Myrtle Johnson, shared along with my long-awaited arrival. He recalled how our father passionately looked upon our mother, as if to sop her up like a biscuit on gravy! Daddy's grand arrival home from work was to swoop mom in his arms, bend her over backwards in a Ginger Rogers and Fred Astaire move and kiss her passionately. It was Dad's way of saying, "Hey Baby Girl, your man is home!"

This was a usual sight to witness; in fact they were always quite affectionate toward each other and their children as well. Richard says our home was like Grand Central Station, having plenty of people, but filled with a lot of love! Even though we didn't have an abundance of material possessions, we had love and commitment, the foundation upon which everything was built in our home.

My mother passed away when I was fifteen-years-old, she died of breast cancer. I did not have the honor of knowing my father; he passed away when I was two years of age. He died from high blood pressure which led to kidney failure. I adored Richard telling me stories of our parents, capturing the residue of their obvious love affair. I was fortunate to see the reflection of my parents' romantic relationship in the marriages of each of my brothers. Naturally, this was to continue in me as well...right? Divorce? Romantic failure? Never in a million years!

Commitment was foundational! I was conceived out of an intense love affair, remember?

I came from a long history of strong men – leaders, so growing up with five brothers was not always easy, but for me, normal. Strength, leadership, and testosterone were no strangers to me. However, their visibility was a constant reminder of protection, and safety, whether all brothers were around or just one. It was clear they had a strong male image to emulate in their lives even long after the cessation of that presence.

My big sister, Dianne, was a mother hen. I was her baby doll; in my formative years, she took me everywhere she traveled. Dianne was a tremendous nurturer with an enormous ability to love people of all types. She hovered over me even after I became an adult with two babies of my own! Oh how I long for those days again, not a single care of my own. Wow, growing up brought life front and center for me.

My sister became very ill, her sickness added to my mounting pressures. It appeared I lost the court battle. I relinquished my new job in Texas for the sake of my children. It appeared I lost my house in Nashville. It appeared he won again. This was yet another pivotal season in my life. And now Dianne's life was ebbing away.

I remember on December 4, 2004, I was standing in line at DFW, waiting to board the plane heading back to Nashville when my sister called me. Her voice was weak, yet her spirit was strong, and her tone was pleasant. Although I lived in a different state, we talked all the time. I would send her calling cards so she could call me anytime, from her home or the hospital. I loved her so much.

Dianne asked if I was on my way to see her and of course I said, "As soon as I land, I'll swoop up my babies and get on the road to Atlanta." We talked for a few more minutes about this, that, and the other, when suddenly there was nothing but quiet. The silence was awkward but golden. I thought perhaps she's in pain and she needs a moment for it to pass which wasn't unusual.

I was utterly unprepared for the next set of words that flowed from her lips, "*I'll wait for you*" she whispered. The quiet was less than a few second, but I tell you, it sure felt closer to minutes; and it was oh so loud. My eyes welled-up with tears. I knew I had better come back with something quick to make this heaviness disappear. When I finally swallowed past the lump in my throat, and pried my lips apart, I blurted out, "*You better, where you think you're going without me?*" Dianne chuckled sheepishly reminding me she's still the oldest although I was the bossy one! Nonetheless, as usual, before every terminated call, we'd say to each other…"*I love you baby… I love you too Dianne.*"

I did not foresee that twenty-three days from standing in DFW airport, my sister's life on earth would end. December 27, 2004, the roles had reversed. I was honored with the privilege to love, protect, nurture and hover over her as she transitioned into the arms of our Lord where suffering was no longer relevant. At the age of 58, my dear sweet sister Dianne Johnson died of colon cancer. I miss her still. I gave her my word I would finish this book…*I did it Sis!*

Our mother was a phenomenal woman. She was beautiful, strong, giving, and graceful. Yes, graceful was a typical word used to describe her. She was an incredible pianist. Richard inherited that particular gift from her. His playing today is just as remarkable. Mom tried to get me interested in piano, but I wanted to skip the fundamentals and play Beethoven without the understanding of the basic scales! (Go figure!)

I reflect on many special memories with my mother. I didn't need the narration of my brothers; I had my own. Mom was in a class of her own, she was jazzy; I didn't understand why she never remarried. This beautiful woman, a widow at 38-years-old with seven children, ranging from 2 to 18 years of age. My brothers and I remember her being pursued by good looking and intelligent men. She was a b-a-a-a-d-d-d girl! (Good 'bad,' off-the-chain 'bad,' fabulous 'bad', Lena Horne 'bad'!) Trust me; having seven children *did not* stop the chase. She was classy and elegant! She didn't walk; she strolled with grace, authority, and a little switch in her hips. Heads turned, mouths dropped, not with lust alone but in awe and respect. (Some say, I walk just like her, my mommy!)

Friends of my parents would say to me, "*Ooh, that Walter James sho'l did love that Myrtle...he used to call her Baby Girl, you know; that was her nickname. You look just like little Myrtle...she was quite the lady. They had a strong love for each other. Anyone who knew yo' folks could see how much they loved each other. Walter James loved his family...yes indeed!*"

I remember at the ripe age of eleven I was preparing to ask my mother questions about my father. We had this sage green, suede-like couch parked in front of the picture window. It was rainy; we were chillin, just the two of us, which was rare, but welcomed. I seized the moment to fire away. Remembering the conversation like it was yesterday, I was determined to have my questions answered – this should be quite simple. Surely, she wouldn't mind answering a few questions. Besides, who could better satisfy my curiosity than mom? According to my brothers, dad wore multiple hats: a husband, father, pastor, business owner and realtor. With all those responsibilities what type of person was he? How did he handle pressure? How did he grow up? Did he have a past? Did he have any secrets? I thought I'd go straight for the jugular and get all the answers I sought.

I had so many questions, I had been given petty answers by others but I wanted to know the real deal. It seemed as my years progressed, the more curious I became about my dad, especially as I interacted with my brothers. There were traits, habits, and attitudes I developed that did not seem to come from my mother.

As Mom sat playing the piano softly, this eleven-year-old girl fired a myriad of questions: "What was daddy like? What kind of person was he? Did you love him a whole lot? Why didn't you marry again? Besides you were only 38-years-old when he passed away. When other men tried to pursue you, why didn't you give them any time, at least a little time, come on?" That's when I got 'the look,' but still I added, "How come I have to grow up without a father?" My beautiful, classy mother looked at me with eyes of warmth, compassion, peace and pain and said, "*Your dad was a good man. He loved me, no doubt about it, and I loved him very much. He was good to us. Through the years we'd always worked things out. We settled our matters privately, behind our bedroom door. You all had one father, which was enough. And even though I was pursued, nobody could take the place of my Walter.*"

To share secrets or past painful experiences was a huge no-no. Secrets were a part of the way things were.

She smiled at me as only she could, then turned her head away to continue playing ever so angelically. I knew she was blinking away tears of remembrance as her words registered in my heart. I watched her missing daddy. Strange as it seemed, I instantly identified with her quiet pain. I too had a void that needed to be filled by that most significant person who was her husband and best friend – my father.

I remember having mixed feelings about what she shared. She gave me the look that said, "*Enough questions today, little girl.*" It's been said that mothers have a third eye in the back of their head. I thought I'd take the risk to ask just *one more* question. As I got ready to open my mouth, I could see that she did not want to talk about it anymore. I should have respected her private feelings of grief, but as I took a breath, Mommy firmly spoke "*Debra Denise!*" Now, whenever I was called by my first and middle name, I knew that meant to 'shut it down, wrap it up, and do so with the quickness'! Yet, she didn't answer my questions completely, which still left me puzzled.

My mother came from the generation that did not talk about certain matters. To share secrets or past painful experiences was a huge no-no. Secrets were a part of the way things were. I was always asking questions. I was good at pushing the envelope. There were missing puzzle pieces inside me. Someone had those pieces but nobody was talking, not even Mom. "What you don't know won't hurt you," the old saying goes. Both parents departed this life with open files to which my siblings and I will never have answers. Perhaps their intentions were to protect us. Obviously revealing the unmentionables was not necessary. "Let by-gones be by-gones" is also a familiar saying. But I was not at peace, I wanted to know why this war inside me was raging.

My mother had a best friend, Mrs. Nola Carthern. Thick as thieves, they held a treasured, rich friendship for umpteen years. Both ladies bore five boys and two girls. If you saw one, you saw the other. Their friendship was admired by numerous people, they truly loved each other. When Mom was diagnosed with cancer, Mrs. Carthern not only had knowledge of this before we, her children did, but she also accompanied her to every appointment, not leaving her side. They shared a bond that anyone would envy, confidantes in the purest form.

Before their friendship was separated by death, Mrs. Carthern (affectionately called Momma Nola) made a promise to look after her best friend's children. Interestingly enough, on my father's death bed she made the same promise to dad to look after his wife and children, which she did. Faithfully, through the years, we all received phone calls, letters, or visits.

When it came time for my wedding day, Momma Nola took a three-day journey on the Grey Hound bus from Sacramento, California, to Detroit, Michigan. She was sick with pneumonia, but she refused to miss my special day. As I prepared to put on my wedding dress, I couldn't help but think of my own mother, desperately wishing she were there. No sooner than the thought surfaced, Momma Nola put her hand on my chin, looking at me as if she were seeing right through me. Eye to eye, she gently stroked my face, and said, "Myrtle would be very proud of you. You've turned out to be quite the lady. My, how much you favor her. Nothing could stop me from being here with you. She loved you so much and so do I. I came to represent her for you because a promise is a promise." We exchanged a moment that felt as if I were gazing into the very eyes of my own mother.

The years had come and gone. The gnawing of the unknown was still, quiet, but not dead. This particular year, I received a letter from Momma Nola that she was coming to visit me! I was very excited for more reasons than one. I was a married woman, an adult, and I couldn't wait to have 'the talk' with her. I had it all planned out. I prepared a list of things to do, places to go, and questions to ask. This was *my* time now. I was ready and prepared to hear the good, the bad, and the ugly.

Three weeks before her arrival, I received a call from her daughter informing me that Momma Nola would not be coming to visit with me after all – she had passed away. "What? No! This can't be! Not again, not her too, this is too much. I don't know how much more I can take!" The word 'shock' does not do justice to what I felt that day. I couldn't find the words to describe this place of agony. It was like repeating the loss of my mother.

I flew to Sacramento, California for her funeral, seeing many old faces. Her funeral was standing room only. I flipped through the program, viewing pictures of her that made me smile, when I heard the preacher say as he eulogized her, "Well, if you knew Nola you knew Myrtle. I believe Myrtle was waiting on Nola at the Pearly Gates, welcoming her best friend home." As I heard those words, I suddenly realized, maybe the emphasis should be on what I know for sure, her love and my parents' strength to endure, rather than dig for something that may possibly bring unwanted and unnecessary discoveries. I realized I was grieving over what I lost, rather than celebrating that which I gained.

Can we do anything about the unknown? No, not really. But we can most certainly recognize there are issues in our lives which must be addressed. We may not be able to pinpoint the direct source, but we may have a general idea of its origin. Those areas that are destructive and unhealthy for us cannot be ignored too long. I promise you it will find its way to your doorstep and expect – in fact, demand – you to let it in. This is not a pleasant subject, and I'm not suggesting you start digging up "dead bones." What I am suggesting is when the issues come across the desk of your mind and place themselves in your face, **do not** ignore them.

You detect these areas in your children and your siblings. You wonder how did "that" find its way to my baby's babies? Generational curses do exist, but so do generational blessings. I teach my children this principle today. When they struggle with something potentially detrimental to their growth as a man and woman, I do not ignore it, I deal with it right then and there. My children will not be ignorant of both families' histories for the sake of pride that could potentially paralyze them as teenagers and adults. More often than not, I get asked by my daughter when she does something crazy, "Mom why do I act like this, where did I get this from?" My response, "You got that from your father's side of the family, of course!" (A little humor, lighten up!)

My parents have been deceased for many years, but I can't help but review my own family with great wonder, *'Who did we get that from?'* speaking of our idiosyncrasies. It's not only possible but probable that every family on this planet has junk – unresolved issues and secrets. It does not matter about your spiritual status, economic status, ethnicity, or creed. The truth is, lies, secrets, habits, and deception do exist. With each passing generation, it continues to grow unless dealt with accordingly. See, in order to truly deal with ourselves, it is imperative for us to go backwards in order to press onward.

My need was to understand myself, my history, my lineage. No, I didn't go hunting for my parents' dirt, but I did recognize different patterns that started to develop, and became more pointed as I grew older. Certain areas seemed to stay on repeat, but why? Why did it take me so long to accept what I knew was a real issue? The truth is some challenges in our lives can lay dormant for years; some areas grow slowly, and others are as clear as the nose on our face. Perhaps if my marriage had not been so messed up, I probably would not have learned the value of walking in this current dimension of transparency.

Conflict, fear, and trust issues woke a sleeping giant from his mountain and it was time to put an end to his existence. My reaction and responses to conflict, fear, and trust, or the nature of it, placed me in a position from which I could no longer run. (Sorry, some things are not for the viewing or listening audience!) However, the road to victory was to first identify these areas and with time, I did. I will tell you this; knowledge is power. It's not so much that we gained knowledge or even how much we retained, but it's what we do with that knowledge and how we applied it to our lives. *That is the key*.

> *It requires maturity and strength to face oneself and take responsibility or ownership for your part.*

To say I wasn't fearful and unsure would be a lie. It requires maturity and strength to face oneself and take responsibility or ownership for your part. You begin to discover areas about yourself that give you a healthy balance and level of truth you did not walk in before. Deception is not necessarily where you traveled previously, but because you operate from a different place in your own mind regarding who you are, now you can better handle and apply the information revealed to you about you.

There is a tendency to want to share with others, longing to invite them over to watch your Discovery Channel, but that is not always wise. Some people have the capability to not let you forget the "you" they encountered. Some have the tendency to discredit you by any means necessary. Trust me; they have their own issues but want you to think yours is more deeply rooted than their own. You just stay the course.

In order to bring healing to those areas a Band Aid no longer suffices for a burned arm. Removing the bandage and applying air and a healing ointment is necessary in order for it to heal properly. A root canal may be an outpatient procedure, but open-heart surgery is not. Realize that your healing process may take longer due to the severity of the operation. Do not try to rush the healing process; you don't want to repeat the surgery unnecessarily.

> *Do not try to rush the healing process; you don't want to repeat the surgery unnecessarily.*

Your desire to walk in wholeness is the first step to healing, and that, my friend, is a good place to start. It can be a quiet place, but it's a great place nonetheless. In the midst of the madness, a still small voice quietly whispers, '*You are better than this*,' and you are. There's a great big world awaiting you to become whole.

You can't move into your future in a state of regret. Cut your losses and move straight ahead.

> *You can't move into your future in a state of regret. Cut your losses and move straight ahead.*

I understood and recognized what it took for me to face the music. I faced it and looked it in the eye and discovered I did not have to carry these weights any longer. As you continue this journey, don't stop! Keep moving! Close your ears to outside voices whether in or outside your home or dwelling. Do not let **anyone** hinder you by bringing up your failures, past or present. You may need to remind people and yourself, it is all in the 'sea of forgetfulness' with a huge NO FISHING! sign posted. Then take their fishing pole and break it! (See Psalm 103:12)

You may be going through a difficult moment right now. Your family situation may not be *The Little House on the Prairie*, or *The Cosby Show*. Perhaps it is more like *The Pursuit of Happyness*, or *Madea's Family Reunion!* The most important thing to realize is the purposes of God will remain in your life; everything you encounter, good, bad or indifferent, really will work out for your good (Romans 8:28). Eventual tragedies and circumstances are utilized to help develop you and build your character. You are stronger than you realize and possibly further along than you envision.

Having said that, it took me many years to comprehend that my destiny was far greater than taking on a renowned married name. I thought this name would redeem me from myself, only to discover the family I married into was just as dysfunctional as the one into which I was born. A 21st century dysfunctional family is not original; this behavior traces as far back as Adam and Eve, the first dysfunctional family after The Fall! You and I cannot dwell in the place of perpetual pain indefinitely. At some point we must recognize it has a purpose. Once pain's purpose is realized, it should

> *You are stronger than you realize and possibly further along than you envision.*

be easier to move forward. Sometimes our mindset is to believe we are addicted to pain and misfortune, but **do not** believe that **lie** anymore.

No matter what your occupation, status or what family you come from or marry into, if there are areas in your life that are challenged (and there most certainly are), or you carry unresolved hurt and frustrated expectations, you must be willing to take the necessary steps to bring closure.

If you are divorced, in a crisis, have failed, or are fearful, rejected, or have been abandoned, nobody can stop your destiny from being fulfilled but you, with God's permission. My destiny was already set in place long before I was a thought in my parents' hearts.

With that being said, we don't get to choose the family we're born into. The last several years of my journey have been quite intriguing. As the smoke began to clear, I sought my family heritage intently. Indeed my family roots were established in rich soil, but some seeds planted – we needed to pray for crop failure!

It is a fact the men in our family were forthright, courageous, driven, proud, stubborn, and at times passive. The human design is not only male DNA, but female as well. I've often said, you can change your mind about many things, but you can't change your destiny, or your family!

Do you see how your family-related issues have affected your life? If so, journal your process.

Is there someone you need to forgive in your family?
Be honest. Keep writing.

JOURNEY THREE

Breaking the Silence

My daughter is my first born. When I saw the ultra-sound indicating I was having a baby girl, I was elated! It's hard to believe she's now almost as tall as me; and to add insult to injury, we wear the same size shoe! Someone said, "There's something in the water." I might have to agree!

Living in this arduous day and time it's essential I keep the lines of communication wide open with my children. I want to know what's stirring in their curious little heads. They are sponges, and I intend to be aware of what they are constantly absorbing.

Miya loves to sit on my vanity and watch me put on my make-up and style my hair. This particular morning, I was preparing to teach a workshop. I typically use these moments of preparation to calibrate my lessons, but Miss Miya decided to indulge me with one of her life's adventures. This baby was talking a hundred miles a minute, non-stop! Timidity had never been an issue for her; that morning she seemed to be chattering with no breaths in between sentences.

Miya's jabber-jawing seemed like the incessant buzzing of a flying insect near my ear. I was zoning in and out of her multiple monologues. When I finally returned to planet earth, the child was still talking! Finally I said, "Miya! Honey! Why are you talking so much this morning?" She said, "Mom, you told me I could tell you anything!" I replied with a gentle, "You're right baby, that's what I said, (sighing softly) continue." And trust me, did she ever!

Oftentimes I chuckle when she asks me questions upon questions; it's like rewinding the tape of my childhood to conversations with my mother… déjà vu! Mommy would give me the same incredulous look I give Miya today. Well, they say, "The fruit don't fall too far from the tree."

The matriarch in me carries the weighty responsibility of preparing my babies for life's realities, disappointments and challenges. Teaching them the importance of being well-balanced is vital. Of course, I can't protect them from everything, but I am driven to instill and teach them principles throughout their lives that build character and integrity. Prayerfully, one day they "will rise and call [me] blessed" (Prov. 31:28 NIV).

Children are a gift from the Lord, indeed. However, when I gave birth, I didn't push out an instructional manual with them! I believe I missed the "How To" parenting class, "Protect Your Kids from Life's Cruelties 101."

Well, life's cruelty for our family manifested in a legal separation, and then divorce; it took its toll on all three of us. Nobody wins in this situation. Unfortunately, the worst repercussions affected my children. There's so much they didn't understand, and even eight years later, I'm still monitoring the effects of that initial tearing. I had to steer the children on a consistent and steady course through this hell. If left emotionally unattended, they would have misinterpreted what was happening.

I had to steer the children on a consistent and steady course through this hell.

The severity of broken families will leave scars at every age. There is a plethora of information explaining the affect divorce has on children whether they have high-profiled parents or not. But protecting my children on every level was my greatest priority. If you mess with my babies; you'll have a war on your hands!

One Sunday, my daughter was waiting for me to pick her up from Children's Church when an adult approached her, *"Hello Miya, you always look so pretty. Listen baby, are your parents divorced?"* "Yes Ma'am," she answered respectfully. The worker announced my arrival; I looked at Miya and sensed something was wrong. As she gathered her belongings she assured me she was okay. My baby girl's silence was making an effort to protect both of our broken hearts. That was not the responsibility of a seven-year-old.

She held this information for months, and later told me she had oftentimes cried herself to sleep; afraid that if she told me 'stuff,' 'the lady' might get in trouble. I taught my children to respect all adults; talking back was not an option if they wanted to live to see their next birthdays! Miya has a tender spirit; she's a vibrant and peaceful child. Her heart's desire is good toward everyone.

One day she and I were having one of our usual chit-chats when she interrupted me, "*Mommy, I want to tell you something, but I need you to promise me you won't snap.*" "*Okay, I promise,*" I said. "MOM!" she emphasized, "*YOU PROMISE?*" "*Yes! I promise.*"

She shared the incident in Children's Church from the months preceding. She saw my fist tighten like Ms. Sophia in *The Color Purple!* Miya pleaded with me not to "smack that lady upside her head!" Although I didn't smack her, I most certainly handled the matter and at the same time assured Miya she was not in any trouble.

The challenge was not addressing the adult; that was the easy part. The real challenge was to determine how long had my daughter carried this pain? I immediately recognized a pattern developing in her that was all too familiar. Miya learned to 'hold stuff' that was emotionally painful to her. She always felt a need to protect her little brother and me. By not 'telling,' she was trying to be a 'big girl' and chose not to burden me with 'one more thing.'

I was adamant about protecting my children from off, stupid, meddlesome, and crazy folk. At the same time, I was just as adamant in dealing with my children's potential character flaws and emotional set backs.

As I said previously, I can't protect them from everything; not even themselves. I have to admit that it alarmed me how well my growing daughter calculated *why* she shouldn't tell me, the *timing* to tell me, as well as the *when* she would tell me. That girl strategically exposed the story when the two of us were just hanging out. Hiding her pain was as natural and easy for her as it was for me in my childhood. I urge my little girl to release her feeling through talking, journaling, writing poems, and songs; which she does very well. To this present day I respect and regard my daughter's thought processes on a deeper and more intimate level. She is me made over. From that situation I pledged to maintain sincere openness with my babies.

The division of two households can be a trip. There are two different sets of rules, two different systems, two different baby-sitters, two different interpretations of the truth, and two different perspectives on what is and is not priority. These are too many variables for children to work through.

The time had come to roll up my sleeves and get my hands dirty. There were developing mindsets and generational patterns attempting to attach themselves to my babies, so part of my journey had ***a lot*** to do with safeguarding the fruit of my womb.

As much as I'm responsible for equipping them for life properly, I couldn't ignore that look in my daughter's eyes as she shared feelings of sadness when asked questions regarding her parents' divorce. This journey now came to a fork in the road I had not fully considered. The children were getting older now, asking more pointed and direct questions, becoming very opinionated, curious of many things as they arrived at their *own* conclusions.

A major transition into the mind of my beautiful daughter became even more noticeable to me while working on my manuscript. Typically my writing time took place when the children were in school or late at night as they slept. Miya came into my room late one night, diving on the bed, scooting next to me to snuggle under my arm. She asked, *"How's it going Mommy?" "Pretty good, Pumpkin,"* I replied. *"Mommy, can I ask you something?* This question became the preamble to profound and penetrating heart issues for my baby girl. *"Tell me the stories about how you grew up, again. Tell me what your mother was like. Tell me how old you were when your mom allowed you to have a boyfriend."*

Sooo, I closed my laptop to tell her the same old stories she had heard a hundred and one times before. My now eleven-year-old, maturing before my very eyes, gazed at me intently and said, "*Tell me more Mommy.*" Her expressions were a mirror of me on that sage-green couch asking my mother to "*Tell me more.*"

Wow! My thoughts were racing. Where do I begin? What can she handle? What is appropriate? What is important? The weight of those gut-punching words unlocked an avalanche of memories, and gave me a unique understanding of the generation that preceded mine.

The weight of those gut-punching words unlocked an avalanche of memories…

The women before me understood their roles as wife, mother, friend, sister, auntie, grandma and most importantly, woman. My grandmothers and great grandmothers were known as pillars in the church and community. They nurtured the sick and shut-in; their homes operated like a hospital as the broken, hurting, and discouraged found refuge and home-cooked meals.

These women where strong, and had a spirit for survival. Wearing multiple hats without thought became second nature. Their dedication to the church goes without saying. The message of the Gospel and church gatherings is how they survived in life. They gave of their time, talents, and treasures, and petitioned the Lord daily anticipating answered prayers.

However, as much as these mothers contributed to their families, church and communities, they learned to master their hidden pain – oftentimes suffering in silence. To them, complaining was a waste of precious time. 'Besides, what goes on in the house, stays in the house 'cause the Lord will fix it all by-and-by!' Airing personal dirty laundry was forbidden. As a matter of fact, their strength was proven based upon the anguish, grief and torment they masked. The underlying demon ultimately was pride. Wearing the Badge of Pride was an honor to that generation. Old folks say, "Bet not tell *nobody* but *God!*"

Unfortunately, what they didn't say or probably didn't know was that their bodies and minds could possibly deteriorate from all those toxins of secrets, fear and pride in their spirits. Transparency can be healing, each time we open our hearts to another wounded soul. Breaking the silence is not shameful if it positively affects another person or generation.

I do not want my children to suffer unnecessarily for lack of information. I intend to prepare them for their journeys. They will have knowledge in hand and wisdom upon their lips. Hopefully, my children will in turn teach their children with added wisdom and perhaps they will turn our world right-side-up!

We must do things differently. Pride will not only stifle our growth but cripple this present generation from recognizing truth and walking in it. It's amazing what you remember when your mind isn't clouded. When you are in a good place spiritually and emotionally, even the unpleasant can be manageable.

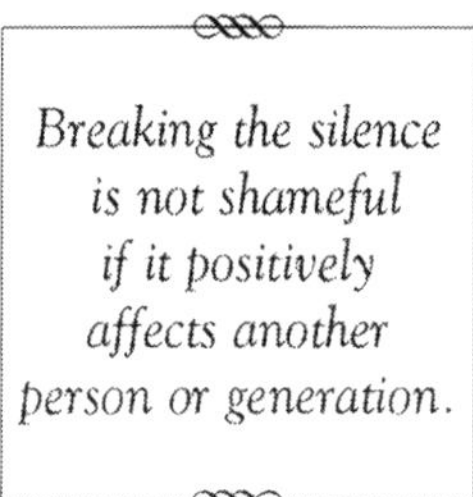
Breaking the silence is not shameful if it positively affects another person or generation.

My mother knew the 'tell me more' of her life, but I was too young to take full advantage of such wisdom. She died too soon for me to appreciate her trials and sufferings as well as her strong faith in the Lord.

One thing that was apparent about my mother was her ability to love and protect her family unconditionally. I wish I knew what transpired in my mom's relationship with her mother that left her unable to communicate sincerely with me. I do know she took deep secrets and wisdom that I needed to her grave.

I wonder if my mother's unconditional love could have been interpreted as misconstrued enablement. Her loyalty to cover and protect those she knew were wrong might have given her a sense of maternal power. I believe this became a disguise in which she herself struggled.

How is it, that loyalty can be confused with enabling? Tainted loyalty can blind one from seeing truth. The moment we decide to keep silent about obvious emotional error in the name of loyalty, we have crossed the line to detrimental enablement. I must confess, I was guilty of such behavior.

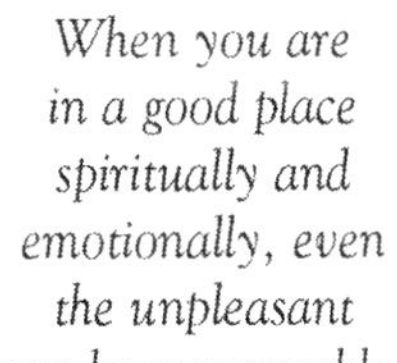
When you are in a good place spiritually and emotionally, even the unpleasant can be manageable.

I shared with my daughter, this little lady packaged in a pre-teen body the importance of not dismissing those things she doesn't like about herself. Both her strengths and weaknesses will help her evolve into the great woman I know she will be. Yet, I pray as she journeys through life I will be there to point out its deceptive schemes. The things I didn't know then, the things no one taught me, and yes, even the things I ignored. Hopefully my experience will be her teacher, not her experience.

It's clear what's been passed on to me: faith, commitment, strength, courage, friendship, honor, tenacity, and vitality, to name a few. But also stubbornness, insecurity, timidity, secrecy and a couple more are added to my list as well. No doubt, my family passed on some mess, drama, iniquitous patterns as all families do, but they also left a Godly legacy, a spiritual heritage of honor and dignity of which I am extremely appreciative.

Unfortunately all families can't say that. My family instilled in me the importance of prayer and maintaining a love relationship with the Lord. I share that with my children as well. I teach them to use the Word of God to combat the enemy of their souls when unpleasant areas arise in their lives. They do not have to succumb to the lies that their family's failures have to be their own.

The moment we decide to keep silent about obvious emotional error in the name of loyalty, we have crossed the line to detrimental enablement.

I may be parentless, but I have been given phenomenal mentors and role models. The Lord in His tender mercies did not leave me motherless. He sent Rev. Ev, a powerful Godly woman who spoke truth and purpose into my life in my early years. She was a woman of great stature who imparted a word of wisdom to me saying, I would not be content doing anything other than what I was created to do. *"It's time for you to launch out into the deep baby, and move into what you're called to do,"* I remember her saying. A relentless demand she required of me. Although Rev. Ev has gone on to be with the Lord, she dutifully passed the baton of truth, wisdom, transparency and wholeness to other spiritual women who keep me on track such as Lelia Harris, Bishop Judy Anderson and Mother Fannie Waters.

My daughter and son, currently reap the same spiritual and relational benefits of not only my matriarchs who have gone on before, but of those who still remain here. We all join hands guiding and teaching our children, but most importantly, we speak truth openly and honestly, breaking the silence.

They do not have to succumb to the lies that their family's failures have to be their own.

How rich is your legacy?

How can you affectively break the silence in your family? What is that family secret that has kept you in bondage?

JOURNEY FOUR

Fact Is, Truth Is

For some time I toiled with writing this book. I'd pick up the pen, write a bit then put it down again. I wasn't quite sure what was appropriate for public knowledge. There were severe battles to overcome. What I did not realize was that the battle was not merely to pen pages, but to experience life a little *more*. I must admit experiencing *more* wasn't all pleasant, but it was essential. To face truth can be a ride in and of itself. Sometimes one can face facts, and not face the naked truth. The saying "truth hurts" is not a complete statement, for truth also heals. The reality is, truth makes you free. However, the responsibility of that freedom will cost you something, and the cost may be associated with hurt. In other words, truth is painful but truth is invaluable.

For example, you're locked in a destructive and debilitating maze in your mind and can't find your way out. In the maze you become claustrophobic, isolated with fears of all sorts rising to the surface. But, there is someone on the outside that has the truth who can guide you to the exit. Follow the instructions you hear to free yourself from that maze, this is your chance for freedom. Truth guides you out of places that have the potential to bring harm and keep you in bondage.

My friend, Dr. Donald Wright taught me the meaning of "It is what it is." This phrase became the foundation of my changing and accepting what I did not want to see or face. He used a simple analogy. "Debra, why are you trying to convince yourself this wall is green when in fact the wall is blue?" The point he was making opened my eyes. I had to stop and realize what it ***is*** rather than what I want it to *become*. The fact is blue is blended with green and yellow; but it's just that, blended. The two colors are not visible to the naked eye, blue is the revealed color.

- The fact is, you were hurt; truth is, it didn't kill you.

- Fact is, you didn't ask for this pain; truth is, you survived anyway.
- Fact is, doctors gave you 6 to 9 months to live; truth is, God determines time.
- Fact is, you had a set back; truth is, it launched you forward.
- Fact is, you are a single parent; truth is, your children are not Fatherless.
- Fact is, you are divorced; truth is your life is not over.
- Fact is, that position was given to someone else; truth is you still have the skills no matter where you're employed.
- Fact is, life isn't always fair; truth is, God will always cause you to triumph.
- Fact is, you lost the battle; truth is, you won the war.
- Facts can change but truth can never be altered!

Hold truth close to your bosom. Wrap truth around you like a warm blanket on a cold windy night.

It's all about how you look at it. Truth can cause one not to take the path of least resistance, but make a painful choice to stop and smell the roses even with the thorns on the stems.

Life's lessons come in assorted packages. We don't always get to pick and choose the paths we travel. However, whatever the path, as long as truth travels with us, we won't miss the mark!

Hold truth close to your bosom. Wrap truth around you like a warm blanket on a cold windy night. Embrace truth, and ***never*** let truth out of your sight.

The principle of truth became more real to me after the passing of my mother; in my journaling it became my conduit for expression. Only a week after her funeral, I was moving away to live with my oldest brother Flynn. It was time to say good-bye to all that was familiar and safe: my friends, my classmates, my church, my neighborhood and my family. I tearfully kissed my sister and other brothers' good-bye as I boarded the plane with Flynn, and his wife Carolyn. We flew from Sacramento, California to Cleveland, Tennessee, my new home (You talkin' about a culture shock!). This was a journey I wasn't quite sure of, but with time I adjusted.

Living life in a fish bowl limits revealing fallible humanity.

Oftentimes, I remember my sister-in-law sharing her heart with me, just needing a safe place to 'dump.' The pressure and challenges of being a wife, mother, pastor's wife, business owner, counselor and the like had been weighty. Yet she knew she had me on whom she could unload, knowing I was a safe ear. Unfortunately, for her, there was no one else at the time. Living life in a fish bowl limits revealing fallible humanity.

Through this, I began to realize I was a safe place as well as a catalyst for emotional healing for others. I was surrounded by women married to men of influence. These ladies were not just in ministry but they were business women, soccer moms, homemakers, and career women.

My sister-in-law conducted meetings with these women. They appeared to share an unspoken bond. Their eyes loudly spoke of private sadness. They discreetly exchanged telephone numbers with one another, having no intent of spilling the beans (of course that's a huge no-no). They were hurting just as much as the folks they counseled weekly and worked with daily. There's an elephant in the room that no one speaks about.

This same sadness was true of some of the men as well. Many were pastors, ministers, bishops, CEOs, CFOs, blue collar workers and successful business men. Is it possible the physician could not heal himself? I remember thinking I wanted to be a person with whom people felt safe to be with, to unload upon, to be transparent with and still keep their self-respect and dignity. I learned early, growing up around ministers and leaders the value of confidentiality and integrity, how to respect the privacy of those who trusted me.

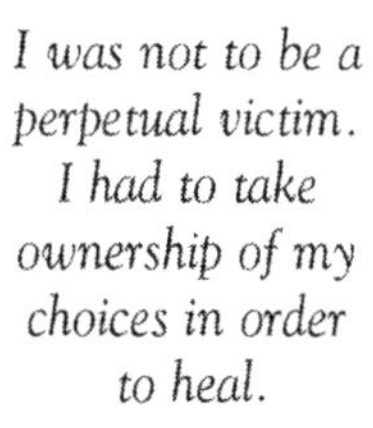

Little did I know, I would marry a man who was a public figure, known around the world. I found myself walking in similar shoes as the ladies I encountered years prior. I remembered the sheer desperation. I was a skeleton in a looking glass. I was bruised and yet, there was a witnessed strength. Although I was an adult, my emotions reflected the pain and agony of that same fifteen-year-old girl who lost her mother years ago. I was very angry. Now, here I was the shoe tightly fitted on my own foot forced to deal with my own stuff, my own issues in truth.

I knew journaling was the one place I could say it all, feel it all, release it all and interpret what I knew to be truth and nobody could stop me or take it from me. Through journaling, I traveled from one destination to another, not taking into account my state of mind. There were no limits to my entries. All things considered, one thing was for sure, I knew I didn't want to be a person who was always hurting, always crying, always finger-pointing. I was not to be a perpetual victim. I had to take ownership of my choices in order to heal. I sought healthy and realistic solutions for myself not realizing I would pass this wisdom on to others.

In retrospect my journaling process illuminated five major areas:

1. It brought to light hidden issues that I was unable to verbalize.
2. It evaluated where I was and how I got there.
3. It defined and re-defined each experience.
4. It righteously deciphered fact and truth.
5. It gave me recognition of my innate ability to cover and protect the soul.

My purpose is to help men and women see themselves through the eyes of the Word of God. I empower people, male and female, to overcome their pasts and encourage them to discover and move forward into their purposes. To me, nothing is more rewarding than seeing someone get it – the "Aha" moment.

As a result of comprehending my purpose, I found freedom! It's like being unplugged. I became unplugged to the voices of doom. I became unplugged to his paralyzing words. I became unplugged to the lie that I was a failure. I became unplugged to the havoc of my past. The source that gave power to all the above had no more energy.

You can plug your ironing cord into the electrical outlet and the surge of power and energy still have access even if the iron is turned off, because its source is still plugged in or connected. But if the cord is disconnected or unplugged from the electrical outlet, there is no more power. It is now powerless, dead, of no effect.

The facts of your life may be substantial, but the truth of who God says you are is irrevocable. Fact is, you may be connected to a devastating past. Truth is, devastation has never stopped God. Why? Because you are not dead...and *THAT'S THE TRUTH!*

Compare what is factual versus what is truth in your life. Then journal how the Hand of the Lord has been with you as you faced this aspect of your journey.

It's amazing where (and how) the Lord shows up, isn't it? Write about it. Even if you did not know it was Him.

JOURNEY THREE

If the Ocean Could Speak

I sure needed this – a time to refresh, to renew, to re-energize my entire being. My writings caused memories to rush to the surface like the waves of the ocean upon which I gazed. The Majestic Beach Towers was appropriately named for indeed I felt like royalty. My dear friends Jim and Caroline Edwards who own this incredible condo in Panama City Beach, Florida, discerned my desperation for seclusion. They knew I needed to unravel deep-seated thoughts, so they offered me their beach front getaway. The view from the 21st floor was magnificent. Wrapped in a champagne-tan blanket, soft as a baby's coverlet, I comfortably stretched out on the recliner on the balcony.

The sun caressed my caramel skin, allowing me to think clearly again. The soft breezes, sugar-white sand and sparkling waters each seemed to applaud me in welcome. This captivated audience of nature encouraged my perception to reach far beyond my imagination.

As breathtaking as the beach and its ocean were this day, I can't help but wonder what lies beneath these calm waves. I thought to myself, "Oh my, if these waters could speak, what stories would they tell?" Imagine the unsolved mysteries. Imagine the priceless treasures hidden under the sea for years and even centuries. The wealth of information enveloped within its depth is invaluable.

We, like the oceans are mysterious and motioning. Our own brilliancy is breathtaking. People may admire our beauty but typically have no clue of our value. Sometimes they have no regard for our hidden treasures within. What we possess is costly, highly respectable, beneficial, marketable and extremely significant. Sometimes we ourselves are ignorant of these facts.

I remember having a conversation with a former in-law. She, strongly opposing the inequitable version of his truth, I tried to convince her I wasn't what he said I was. I felt I must make this point, because she must be told the truth! I felt like I was in a court of law as I defended myself. As I litigated my innocence I heard these words resounding in my ear. *"She does not validate your life, I DO!"*

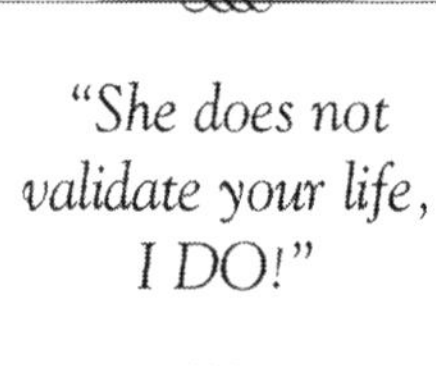

I stopped speaking in mid-sentence. I will never forget that day. It was obvious I had been visibly shaken. No need to argue my case, I chose to dismiss myself from her presence. With no explanation or further discussion, I swiftly walked out the door. I cried all the way home, feeling like an idiot for allowing myself to succumb to her opinion of me. I asked the Lord to forgive me for wanting man's approval more than His. From that day to this, I never entered into another debating session pertaining to who I am.

Mankind opens its eyes to nature with a profound thought, 'There is a God!' The Omnipotent One commands the boundaries of the oceans and they obey. He says, "This far and no further." At His word alone, He commands the roars of the seas to quiet, and they submit. Fitting to the very nature of the seas to obey His every command, every creature follows suit. Interestingly enough, there were no classes offered on how to be a shrimp, crab or whale. The tropical fish did not ask other fish if the colors assigned to them coordinated well with their fin structure! My point is simple, every creature God created functions in the purpose of its original design without the opinion of others.

We human beings ask men to tell us who we are instead of asking the One who created us in the very image and likeness of Himself! We search the earth looking for someone to follow, someone to validate us, to tell us the purpose of our existence. And if we don't find it, we conjure up our own crazy philosophy that makes no sense whatsoever as we end up living out a lie. Then, it takes years to undo what **we** did to ourselves!

I believe our existence is just as significant as that of the fish in the sea. You and I were hand crafted by God Himself – The Creator of all universes! That's serious stuff! As a matter of fact, Psalm 8:5 NLT declares, "*For You have made him (man) a little lower than the angels, and You have crowned him (man) with glory and honor*" *(parenthesis mine)*.

That means, just as sea creatures are given a purpose, everything He created has a purpose – a divine purpose – and that includes you and me. It further means that if I want to know about how and for what reason I was designed, then I must inquire of the Master Designer! Better yet, God claims the indisputable right to do as He wills with those who belong to Him. (I hear you thinking) "You mean to tell me there are treasures inside of me that have gone undiscovered?" "Are you suggesting there's more to my life than the drama I've experienced?" The answer is a resounding Yes!

In my opinion, I believe one of our greatest offenses toward the Lord is not fulfilling our purpose. Not believing in yourself is offensive to God. Not believing in the very thing you have a passion for which He put in you to complete, you're suggesting God didn't know what He was doing or maybe He made a mistake when He created you. God is too wise to make a mistake. It is God who gives us daily permission to breathe His air! Logic says the Creator of this universe who carefully structured and handcrafted the fish of the sea, the fowl of the air, and every creeping thing that creeps and crawls on the earth (Gen. 1:21-22 NLT) took just as much, and even more pleasure and thought in creating us.

Each one of us was carefully crafted in His image and in His likeness. If you're going to imitate anyone, imitate Jehovah God the Author of all things! Listen to this: God is so in love with you, He actually sings over you! You don't believe me? Look at Zephaniah 3:17 KJV, ***"The Lord thy God in the midst of thee (you) is mighty; he will save, he will rejoice over thee (you) with joy; he will rest in his love, he will joy over thee (you) with singing"*** (King James Version, parenthesis mine).

In other words, He is a mighty Savior. He delights in you with gladness. He displays His expression of His affection toward you. It gives Him pleasure to serenade over you as a groom to his bride. You are always on His mind as well as upon His lips!

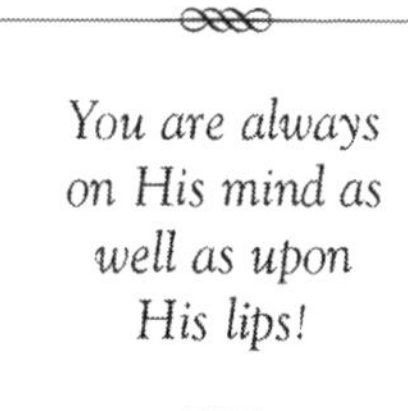
You are always on His mind as well as upon His lips!

The oceans of this planet are far-reaching. Its depths and discoveries are beyond imagination. The oceans of your life are full of treasures. God knows everything there is to know about you. Contrary to popular opinion, your "oceans" are filled with greatness. You are not shallow; the riches inside you are immeasurable. If your life's ocean could speak, what treasures would you or someone else discover? Will the real you please come forward? If you had the platform, what would you say? Would you take that opportunity to get even or change someone's life? Why not start by changing your own life? Launch out into your deep and get moving. Your hidden treasures anticipate your coming! You are immersed in greatness!

Every challenge of life has its smoke screens and convincing distractions; they can leave you in a place of motionless agony. What you must remember is all sickness ain't unto death! Life is altered, not over!

If nothing up to this point has convinced you, hopefully the written Word of God will. Check this out!

"O Lord, you have examined my heart and know everything about me. You know when I sit down or stand up. You know my every thought when far away. You chart the path ahead of me and tell me where to stop and rest. Every moment you know where I am. You know what I am going to say even before I say it, Lord. You both precede and follow me. You place your hand of blessings on my head. Such knowledge is too wonderful for me, too great for me to know! I can never escape from your Spirit! I can never get away from your presence! If I go to heaven you are there; if I go down to the place of the dead, you

are there. If I ride the wings of the morning if I dwell by the farthest oceans, even there your hand will guide me, and your strength will support me. I could ask the darkness to hide me and the light around me to become night - but even in darkness I cannot hide from you. To you the night shines as bright as the day. Darkness and light are both alike to you. You made all the delicate, inner parts of my body and knit me together in my mother's womb. Thank you for making me so wonderfully complex! Your workmanship is marvelous and how well I know it. You watched me as I was being formed in utter seclusion, as I was woven together in the dark of the womb. You saw me before I was born. Every day of my life was recorded in your book. Every moment was laid out before a single day passed. How precious also are your thoughts about me, oh God! They are innumerable! I can't even count them; they outnumber the grains of sand! And when I wake up in the morning, you are still with me! Psalm 139:1-16 (NLT)

And **that's** the conclusion of the matter!

What are you robbing the world of by hiding who you are?

What is the purpose of your existence? Hey, you may not know today, but think about it, then write about it.

JOURNEY SIX

Betrayal and Forgiveness

The General's Daughter is a fictional story of betrayal and unforgiveness. The general's daughter Elizabeth, a high-ranking officer in the military was head of the Psychology Special Operations department. Her eminent athletic and academic ability out-ranked the entire platoon. She was the best in everything she set out to accomplish, but her father continually seemed not to acknowledge, congratulate or encourage her.

Elizabeth's ambition, like most daughters, to do and be the best was motivated by receiving her father's approval. During training at West Point, Elizabeth was beaten and ganged-raped by several men in her unit. After the incident her father was summoned by his superior officer who informed him of the rape of his daughter and its severity. Because her father was on the verge of a promotion to general, his superior officer suggested he take into account his advancing career in the military. This suggestion would be best for all involved; the army didn't need a scandal of this magnitude publicized. Elizabeth's father wanted justice for his daughter's sake, of course.

He was devastated when he entered her hospital room and saw the affects of the cruelty inflicted upon his own flesh and blood. But for the supposed greater good, it was highly recommended her father inform his own daughter to act as if the rape and assault never happened. He instructed his daughter to close her eyes and rest, be at peace, and pretend this horrible incident never occurred. She reluctantly agreed this was the best decision for all involved; that everything would be just fine and to trust her father as she always had. As instructed Elizabeth closed her eyes slowly in terror, confusion and disbelief. His daughter was not at peace neither did she forget.

As traumatic and devastating as rape is to a woman the most vile violation was now happening. Elizabeth's father neglected her traumatic experience for the sake of his own promising career. A line in the movie even more emphatically states, "*There's something far worse than rape and assault...betrayal!*"

Elizabeth went through years of counseling; she learned to bury her pain deep inside, believing the façade she was over the incident. She pulled her exterior self together and continued with a successful career in the psychology department. With accrued authority and achievements under her belt, Elizabeth manipulated and controlled officers with the same level of power as her father, but for her own sensual pleasure. Each conquest was a sad attempt to fill a void within.

> *Pain is real; nobody should tell you not to feel it but misplaced or mismanaged pain can be dangerous.*

Power to Elizabeth was like putting Band-Aids on gaping wounds. The accomplishments did not give her the attention she sought from her father; in fact, she was more angered by his approval of her success. It was her need for the general to be a parent that Elizabeth actually sought. Her behavior became destructive and that behavior led to her demise. The general betrayed his own heart, the love of his daughter, for the sake of climbing the military ladder. Unfortunately, that betrayal is what destroyed Elizabeth's broken spirit.

Although this is a fictional story, and more than likely extreme; the similarities are quite relevant. We trust those who say they love us not to inflict harm on us in any way. When pain is executed by someone we love, it is our nature to react. Pain is real; nobody should tell you not to feel it but misplaced or mismanaged pain can be dangerous.

I believe how we handle that pain or hurt, and where we place it in our psyche becomes the relative issue. In Elizabeth's case, she held on to her pain for vindictive reasons that were justifiable in her mind. But at the end of the day, what she felt justified in resulted in her death. Although she had columns of stripes and medals, she was far from mentally and emotionally balanced.

Sadly, forgiveness was not exchanged by any guilty party and every party was guilty.

Do I think some people betray with the intention to destroy? Unfortunately, yes. However, for whatever warped reasons there are for such behavior, intentional betrayal is without excuse. It's a known fact that hurting people hurt people. Please hear me, I am in no way trying to diminish your hurt, but I am saying don't let it control you to the point you become lethal to yourself, your family or to the world at large.

In my case, my mother's last request was for my oldest brother Flynn to raise me as his own. My brother becomes my father-figure. Now, here I was caught between the roles of sister, daughter, baby-sitter to his children, and administrator to his business. The predicament in my mind was how to juggle each role; I struggled to fit into not one, but all categories. This revealed itself in my teenage rebellion, and as a young woman who made poor decisions that led to a few unhealthy relationships. I don't believe my brother knew the impact of raising his baby sister while trying to raise his own family. Regrettably, I became the source of contention in his household.

This little girl, this young woman more than anything, was on a quest for a place called 'her own.' My brother loved me, I knew he did. He was keeping a promise to raise me in a manner our mother would have been pleased, and through trial and error, he did. He was trying to keep everything a float; his marriage, his ministry, his business, and me.

The other side of his commitment to our mother's request involved me living with his family. That request included my sister-in-law taking on a responsibility she had not anticipated. This experience for me was the beginning of years of confusion, pain and the uncertainty of my future. Feeling the separation of my mother's love and safety left me in despair. Only tears could fill the place of my mother's missing love.

It was in this period of time where the pain of loss, rejection, abandonment and oftentimes hopelessness began to fuel a breeding ground of bitterness and unforgiveness. It showed up throughout my life. I was looking for and still longing to be mothered at fifteen. That place in my heart was still painfully empty; this desire of mine became a source of irritation and pressure to my brother's wife. Through many years of struggles and even times of joy, my emotional needs changed. I didn't need to replace my mom or her love; I needed to change my expectation of my sister-in-law. I had to accept the fact she didn't have the ability to give me my mother's love. The conflict in the relationship that still remains is no longer within me. In retrospect, there were life lessons I probably would not have learned had it not been for her firm methods of rearing. In spite of everything we've been through, I must thank her for accepting a role she could have refused.

> *When people hurt you, you feel they should be punished, yes?*

The wounds of rejection are painful whether inflicted deliberately or not. But I had to learn I couldn't begin to heal my heart and mind if I had not made a conscious decision to forgive and release her from the debt I believed she owed. I did not understand the motive or intent of the pain she inflicted. The truth is my choice not to stay bitter was very difficult. Either way I am responsible for the condition of my own heart. But the reward of canceling debts, releasing my rights and forgiving was like parasailing. The fresh air blew through my hair and the sun beamed upon my face. I call it freedom.

When people hurt you, you feel they should be punished, yes? Should they pay for their injustices? How about a public apology on CNN or even the local news would be a good start? No, not really. The truth is they can't repay you. They can't restore that which has been damaged and broken. Only the Lord can redeem the unredeemable.

> *Only the Lord can redeem the unredeemable.*

Life happens and we all experience mishaps and ship wrecks. But hidden from the range of the enemy, we have the best gift ever – Forgiveness. It is a gift, not a right.

You have the right to fight back, you have the right to get even; you have the right for your side to be heard, you have the right to your own opinion; that is your right. However, rights come with an expected return. When it's all said and done, after you rehearse what you have rights to, how will you deal with your internal issues? Will you hold that person or persons hostage since you will not release and forgive them? Forgiveness is your gift to give away to the very ones who damaged or almost crippled you. Will the scars remain? Probably, but they are healing reminders that you came through. Will you remember? Sure you will, but without the venom as your bedfellow. Should they pay? The reaping and sowing principle applies to us all (Galatians 6:7).

At the age of innocence, the purpose of unforgiveness is to wildly fester. It hopes you never ever find the solace of recovery and freedom which in actuality lay prostrate at your feet. Sometimes trouble comes to drive you to your knees, and this place of submission is the best position for recovery.

Forgiveness is your gift to give away to the very ones who damaged or almost crippled you.

The pitfalls of life and all their smoke screens are designed to keep us in total darkness. But dear friend, there's nothing like coming into the knowledge of the truth. Truth is like the chemical that destroys fires!

Truth is equivalent to a table set for fine dining, spread with beautiful china and crystal stemwear. First class, white-gloves and silver platter service! Truth is like being the guest in an exclusive hotel with wonderful amenities, prepared for the royal spa treatment that's indescribable. Resting in total bliss on the best mattress ever, knowing your history of back pain and insomnia. Your room is exquisite and elegant, Godiva chocolates, and strawberries await your indulgence. The aroma of freshly cut flowers greets you in every room. Imagine it, five-star treatment! Oh, I'm sorry; I failed to mention your five-star living quarters are in the middle of the Sahara Desert! I didn't say discovering truth was always found in the center of fabulous locations!

Even though I was awakened by the truth of who I am, I was still stuck in the swirling stench of the cesspool of my current situation. I was still in the midst of battles for my life, my children, my destiny, my purpose and my peace. The magnificent revelation of truth and forgiveness enabled me not only to survive; but to live a purposeful life that underlined forgiveness of myself and others. Where there is truth – forgiveness must follow.

Betrayal is deadly, but forgiveness is the source that permeates life. This gift you possess is not a one-time deal; it's for a lifetime, and should be distributed daily. Forgiveness is for you as much as it is for the perpetrators – perhaps even more. Make it your life's ambition to give forgiveness away in a world that is cold and heartless. Sow the gift of forgiveness, the return is heavenly!

Have you ever been betrayed by someone you cared a great deal about? Write it.

Are you ready to forgive them, yes? Share how you will do so. If not, why?

JOURNEY SEVEN

Everyone Needs a 'Samwise Gamgee'

Alright, I confess, I'm a movie buff! Have you seen *The Lord of the Rings*? Frodo Baggins, Samwise Gamgee, and the Shire? Really, you should watch the entire series; there are numerous principles to glean. I deliberately focused on the friendship between Frodo and Sam. Frodo's assignment given from the good wizard was to save middle earth by destroying the Ring of Power that was designed to destroy the shire. Sam's assignment was to protect Frodo at all cost, as they traveled by foot on an extraordinary and life-threatening journey. They both accepted their assignments, but had no clue what to expect in their travels. Through blood, sweat, and tears, they learned the value and honor of friendship. These two unlikely people through their commitment to each other stood the test of time for the greater good.

The journey was frightening as they faced many days of uncertainty, yet they pressed on. The closer they came to "their destination" the more difficult the journey became. Tired, weary, and worn, they came across a little creature named Sméagol. Its appearance seemed innocent and helpless, but it was far from either one. Sméagol became a nagging, manipulative presence tagging along to keep them from reaching their destination. It had a hidden agenda, it wanted one thing and one thing only...the Ring of Power that was to be destroyed. Sam immediately recognized this presence (Sméagol) as a distraction, but Frodo did not – hmmm?

Many long hot days passed and the nights seemed more frightening as Frodo grew exhausted from the long trip. He became physically and emotionally weak, not remembering the taste of food or water when he fell limp in Sam's arms. In Frodo's state of exhaustion, his memory grew faint. Sam began to rehearse to Frodo the scenery of his home – the shire, and seasonal flowers blooming and the taste of strawberries, but Frodo could not remember it. Throughout this journey Sam could sense how weighty this task had become for Frodo and he knew Frodo was at his end. Yet dear Sam mustering all his strength said, *"I can't carry it for you, but I can carry you! Come on Mr. Frodo."*

Oh my, what a statement! Sam physically put Frodo over his shoulders and carried him to the entrance of their destination. He understood middle earth would be destroyed if Frodo did not fulfill his assignment. Middle earth hadn't realized it was depending on Sam just as much as it was depending on Frodo. More importantly, Sam's love warranted no price, a promise was a promise.

"Greater love has no man than this, than to lay down one's life for his friends."
(John 15:13)

Accomplishing the task through adversity, the two friends exchanged a gaze of unspoken affection and gratefulness for the other. Frodo exhaustively acknowledges his gratitude for having Sam with him at the end of all things.

"Greater love has no man than this, than to lay down one's life for his friends" (John 15:13 NLT).

I traveled the road alone often. Pivotal seasons were accompanied by extraordinary friends. Each person had a measured time and space. Each person played a significant and strategic role for that particular place. Some relationships were short-lived, but necessary. Other relationships seem to have been a part of my life for a substantial amount of time, but in reality a few years or so may be more accurate.

Then you have the 'stick closer than a brother' friends, 'the long haulers.' I like to refer to them as 'keepers,' pledging to walk with you down *The Green Mile*. Lest I forget, our faithful, fair-weathered friends who make the complexity of life just a little more complex! Some friends walk close, others walk closer or not at all.

"Where you're destined to go, determines who goes with you," it is said. It is also said, "People come into your life for a reason, season or a lifetime." I wholeheartedly agree.

We are each in need of someone to understand our assignment and more than that, help fulfill it. Such a person or persons are designed to guard the doors of your destiny and keep the unwelcomed out. Heroes like Sam are rare, but I can attest they do exist.

Even the wisest of men understood this principle. In 1Kings 4:1-6 King Solomon was choosing his officials for his administration. Each office was given a title to the designated head of that office, such as Court Secretaries, Commander of the Army, and Palace Administrator.

Acquaintances are common but authentic friendships are rare.

But the particular office that caught my attention was, "The Trusted Advisor and Friend to the King." The king valued friendship so much, he made friendship an office. That's unbelievable! King David taught his son Solomon this principle of accountability and friendship. King David's friend and trusted advisor Nathan, who ironically was the father to King Solomon's friend and advisor, Zabud! What a wonderful principle to pass on to your children!

Other references of deep friendships are Jesus and His disciples, David and Jonathan, Naomi and Ruth, Oprah and Gayle, Celie and Nettie, and my mom and her friend, Myrtle and Nola. Acquaintances are common but authentic friendships are rare.

By far, the friendship journey is the most paramount and lengthy journey that we share. No man is an island unto himself. The real challenge is thinking we can heal ourselves by ourselves whether due to our independent nature, being too prideful to ask for help, or even the obvious, a major lack of trust. This is a continual battle for both male and female.

How do you decipher what category of 'friend' people are in your life? Are they keepers, fair-weathered, covenant, or perhaps friendly acquaintances? There are several ways to decipher friendship levels, but what has proven true for me is, the saying "time reveals all things." I learned time is my friend, not my enemy. Time allows all parties involved to see what's authentic and what's not. We all can be impatient with time, but as my mother declared years ago, "*Keep living baby, put a little time on it you'll see.*"

Life's journey awards no guarantee that a person or persons will remain your friend for a lifetime. But experiencing enough of life will test the portal of time that proves through it all, those friends which remain.

The Sméagols, or distractions in life are essential. They too have their place. Michael Corleone's (*Godfather III*) philosophy was, "*Never hate your enemies it clouds your judgment.*" I didn't learn this lesson well initially. I reacted to the behavior of other's stupidity, thinking if I gave them a piece of my mind or discredited them openly it would make *me* look better in the eyes of those I thought mattered. I was grossly mistaken.

I learned time is my friend, not my enemy. Time allows all parties involved to see what's authentic and what's not.

Genuine friendships are worth fighting for, but it is never a one-sided duel. I can't emphasize this point enough. Please, do not allow outside forces or distractions in the form of people to interfere with your relationships; regardless of the level, you must protect them. Make sure you confront and deal with those who are the cause of the interferences immediately. Open your eyes and do not ignore the signs of interferences. Anything worth having is worth fighting for.

Good relationships for me have stood the tests of time. Inevitably, as the years pass, the needs change in each one. As in marriage, needs change. What you needed at age twenty-three is different at age thirty-three, forty-three, fifty-three and so forth.

Discerning the change of times and needs requires us to make necessary adjustments to maintain that relationship. If we do not, we run the risk of losing the relationship all together. Consequently, people change and so do we.

We must continually change the way we think, for behind everything we do is a thought, every behavior is motivated by a belief, and every action is prompted by an attitude.

Adjusting, letting go, moving on, making mistakes, friction, growth and so much more are all parties to the process of change. Difficult at times, yes; but necessary nonetheless. To resist change is a waste of time and energy, for it is a part of living on this earth. We must continually change the way we think, for behind everything we do is a thought, every behavior is motivated by a belief, and every action is prompted by an attitude.

Friendships are priceless treasures. Having a good support system keeps one accountable, sane, and balanced. Catch a glimpse of my treasured friendships, each are rare and priceless. These jewels have names: Regenia, Stephanie, Charlene, Cynthia, Lee, Darryl, Craig, Sylvia, Pam, Elaine, Lisa and Richard and Veronica.

Regenia Knight:
The Optimistic Listener

Nearly a thirty-year friendship, "Gena" has been with me through every aspect of my life from obnoxious teenager to the arrival of my first child, and even to this present day. With a few hundred miles between us, we had no problem keeping Bell South in business. Our relationship is quite unique. It's safe to say out of all my friendships, we've probably spent less time together than any of the others. But most unique, is our eleven-year age difference. Not only is she a seasoned woman, but she prays for me and she carries me close to her heart. My personal cheerleader for many years, Gena encouraged me to write this book and to continue training others in leadership along with the platform of conference speaking. Thanks to her today, I still function in both those capacities. We've walked with each other through some "sho' nuff stuff."

I believe Gena was probably the most patient with me for many reasons. Her temperament is calm; she is overall a patient person. The fact that Gena is a phenomenal teacher adds to her ability to break life-lessons down and biblically build precept upon precept. Her quiet persistence kept me from making hasty, emotionally-driven decisions which in hind sight would have been catastrophic.

Gena is also an intense listener. Those tangent days when I was determined not to listen to anyone, including her, she knew how to call my name, as if I had heard it for the very first time, quieting my roaring soul. Today we laugh about how crazy I was. Yet, she would consistently understand and forgive my actions. I remember her saying, *"Deb, it's okay, I know you're angry and hurting right now. But one thing I know about you, when the smoke clears, you always come back to yourself and do what's right! You are a strong woman Deb, very strong; you're going to be just fine, watch and see what I tell you."*

Gena saw the best in me in the worst of times. As a matter of fact, she took it upon herself to do a word study on the meaning of my first name. It was an amazing eye-opener for me. I discovered my name is what I do and who I am! Gena always said I was a strong leader and bossy now she had proof…it's a part of my name! Thank you Gena, for not jumping ship when it looked like I was about to shipwreck.

Words from Gena:
I have known Deb as I affectionately call her, for 28 years. At our initial introduction there was not an immediate connection because I thought she was t-o-o-o-o bossy! From that time until now, I have come to know her as a compassionate, loving friend. We have shared long hours of conversation on the phone (she's an excellent listener). One of my greatest memories of Deb is how she helped me through a rough time after my second child. I needed help in so many areas and without a warning a few days later, she came to visit and lent support

to me and my family. We have been through good times as well challenging times, and our friendship has stood the test of time.

I must say that Deb has been very patient with me over the years. There have been times that I have good intentions to send information to her that has taken weeks. (For instance the information for this book!), and her reply has always been, "Gena please don't forget." I am truly glad that she has not given up on me because she sees my heart. I have many great memories in my friendship with Deb; I could go on and on.

Stephanie Fitzgerald:
The Rock

I was a wreck. One big sobbing mess! I was sitting on the floor in my office preparing for divorce court. I said to Stephanie, "*Who will ever want me with two babies? What man won't be intimidated by my married name?*" Stephanie looked at me with a piercing, glaring stare. She could have whipped me like one of her children when she said, "*WHAT? What did you say to me? Girl, I ought to hit you with this note pad! Let me tell you something about you....*"

Intensely, she began to articulate the type of woman I am. She took the power out of my curse-filled words by countering with, "*That's a lie from hell! He did not value you, it's his loss, wait and see what God will do, God is up to something, you're not walking through this for nothing, people need to know there's hope and they need to hear what you have to say!* (Taking a quick breath she continued) "*Look, I understand you may have to walk through these different emotions but I* ***will not*** *let you be crazy, I* ***will*** *reel you back in!*" (Fussing softly under her breath) "*I still ought to hit you for thinking like that...who will want you?...please...!*"

Stephanie was my voice of reason, my anchor of sanity in my sea of perplexity. She still is. We have had countless conversations. Stephanie is well acquainted with me, this 'funky-mood-bad-attitude-mad-at-the-world-mad-at-the-church-emotional-roller coaster-no-makeup-bad-hair-day (which, by the way, was often)-talking-out-of-both sides-of-my-mouth,' sistah. A woman of faith one moment, Doubting Thomas the next! Whew, I was all that!

Consensus suggests taking one day at a time; I was doing well to take one moment at a time. Yet, she never rushed me, but she wouldn't let me stay in that place of instability too long. Steph was a rock. She remains that rock today. She accompanied me to every court appearance. Once we were in arm's reach of the "enemy" but she kept her cool, not allowing Compton to show up in her in Nashville! (That's an inside joke).

We watched the whirlwind of drama that's associated with divorce court. Knowing me oh-too-well, Steph knew I was absorbing everything my eyes captured. She would veer my attention away by distracting me to something humorous, like a comical fashion faux pas, or a court employee going about his duties in a comical manner.

My dear sister and friend carried me from one point to the next. I collapsed in her arms many times from my heavy burdens. Yet like Samwise Gamgee, she continually reminded me of my assignments in the earth. The times when I was not thinking clearly she would put her arm around me, cry with me, and speak with her eyes only, "I'm here. I got you." Even as I reminisce today, tears fill my eyes realizing the depth of friendship in Steph. I don't know how she found the time, caring for a husband and five children, but she did. Thanks Steph, indeed you're the wind beneath my wings!

Words from Stephanie:

"Having Debra as a friend for the past 10 years has meant a lot to me. She has been a consistent, reliable, faithful, and crazy friend. I have been able to laugh, cry, be silly, be angry, and be stubborn, and on occasion all at the same time! Nonetheless, Debra has allowed me to be me and love me just the same. She has believed with her whole heart who God has created me to be and she refused to sit back and allow me to be anyone less than who God has said that I am. She pushes me toward greatness. She has a gift for knowing when to be firm and when to back off and let me work it out. Her famous word to me were "O.K. Boo, a-l-r-i-g-h-t" and the whole time she would be thinking 'Now you know you're acting crazy.' She has been faithful to our friendship and to my family. Debra believes in the vision that God has not only for me but for my family me. My children love their Auntie

Debbie mainly because she keeps them out of trouble and from completing their school work! I am blessed because Debra is my sister not just my friend."

Charlene Beard:
The Motivator

Charlene is my cheerleader, motivator, educator and sounding board. She's a keeper! When I speak of Charlene, I always tell people I want to be just like her when I grow up! Charlene has a brilliant mind with the tenderest heart of compassion. She believes I can do anything but fail. She is the rope that I hold onto, better yet, she's the knot at the end of the rope. Charlene would not turn me loose.

I'll never forget the day we made an impression of friendship; she too experienced a painful divorce. One afternoon we sat at a restaurant talking for hours about my life, about her life, and about our current legal matters. We had not known each other on this deeper level very long.

I vividly remember looking into her despairing eyes and thinking, "This woman is incredible but she doesn't know it." She was hurting too bad to see worth.

We talked and talked, unsure what the future held not only for her but for either of us. That was more than five years ago. Presently, girlfriend is the Global Senior Staff of Human Resource at General Motors and doing it! Contrary to the opinion of others, she is a better woman, after divorce not a bitter one. And to top it off, she is one of my closest and cherished friends and one of my most favorite people.

Charlene Beard inspires me! She prays for me. She pushes me beyond myself and demands I think out of the box. When we work on projects together, we are a force to be reckoned with. Between me popping sunflower seeds in my mouth and her guzzling Sprites, we are unstoppable! Charlene brings a rare brilliancy to our friendship that's priceless. You are all that and then some, you go Girl!

Words from Charlene:

"I've heard that "the greatest tragedy in life is not death, but life without purpose, and it is more tragic to be alive and not know why you live." Debra's friendship to me, our candid discussions and her natural ability to genuinely get to the heart of matters has catapulted me into areas of my divine purpose that I didn't realize existed.

Debra has literally walked me through some of the most darkest moments of my life until I could see the light...I'll always be thankful for that...God forbid; who knows, I may not have made it!

Debra's friendship to me...Our friendship together is Life With Purpose!

Cynthia Williams:
The Realist

Cynthia is an intelligent and brilliant person. She is straight forward, what you see is what you get period! You will <u>never</u> have to second guess her. Yet, as straight forward, opinionated, and unpretentious as she is; Cynthia's ability to go above and beyond the call of duty is something she prefers to keep under the radar. Her disposition is unassuming and rather misunderstood. Yet, Cynthia always zeros in on the one in need who oftentimes appears unnoticed. More than likely, she will find a way to meet that person's need.

I remember my early years I was a baby-sitter for my brother's children, and an administrator for their business and church affairs. In the midst of my multiple duties, one day Cynthia walked up to me with a question that angered me but caused me think. She said, "So, Debra, what do you want to do with your life?" My reaction accompanied a pious attitude, "What do you mean? I'm doing it?" She continued. "I don't mean for your brother, I mean for you – your future." I rolled my eyes at her as I continued with my responsibilities not saying a word. My horrific attitude didn't faze her in the least. Cynthia would return the next week expecting an answer.

I cannot tell you how angry I was with her. Why angry? Because I didn't have a answer for either of us. Strangely enough, that's when our friendship began. Somehow she'd seem to find her way into my presence, and begin pulling at my quiet dreams deep within me. Cynthia often notified me I had much to offer and that God was requiring those things He put in me to come forth.

A few years passed when we became room mates. We had the best time. At any given moment, we'd jump in her gold two-seater Toyota taking a road trip, here-there and everywhere. Boy, we have stories to tell! We shared numerous times of laughter, weary-times, broke-times and times of abundance. Our lives have gone in different directions; we've gone months without touching bases but when we talk, we pick up as if we lived a few blocks away.

Cynthia is the real-deal. I respect her and her multiple giftings. She's an original design and voice of encouragement and reason; reminding me it's my time. "Now is your time Deb, now is your time." Thank you for being there in the midst of…it ALL!

Neutral has no voice…

Words from Cynthia:

Debbie has been the person that God put in my life who inspired, motivated, corrected, and encouraged me throughout our relationship. She was the first person in my life to help me understand that I was fearfully and wonderfully made. She helped me learn that logic is not always God's answer to a problem. Above all things, our relationship remains because Debbie truly exemplifies the very essence of the meaning of agape love…and she's my friend for life!

Unfortunately, there are those relationships, which do not stand the test of time. Some choose to love from a distance. To be associated with me while I'm in the thick of things may cramp their style. Remaining "neutral" worked best for them, but left me wondering. Neutral has no voice; its position is a safe stance. Friends don't take sides; friends stand for truth. This side of relationships was very agonizing and hurtful for me, I just didn't get it – and I still don't. I am a loyal friend. I don't know how to love half-way; for me, it's all or nothing. When my friends need me, I'm there without question, so the lack of response, from some friends was unexplainable to me.

You know how it works with these folks. In your presence their loyalty is evident and clear. But how can one be on your side while they are by your side, but leave your side and yo' butt is left outside? Now that's the mystery baby! Unavoidably, the loyalty of a relationship will be tested. That is when you discover what the relationship is honestly made of. Pressure will blow your cover, remember?

I felt stuck, angry, and betrayed.

Regrettably, amnesia sets in. Now, for whatever reason they don't want to be "involved." You have been sold out; and it hurts deeply. Cut off and isolated from the Friendship Club, the silence speaks volumes, while left to face every negative emotion imaginable, all alone. True, not everyone can handle the intimacies and intricacies of relationships. However, it is always respectful to communicate where you are, what you can or cannot contribute to the relationship in total honesty, not convenience.

For me, this was agonizing. It was difficult to pull myself up by my bootstraps. I could not fake it; I was seriously knocked off balance. I felt stuck, angry, and betrayed. More importantly with time, I learned many profitable lessons that would catapult me through the journey of life with much needed wisdom. I was not out of the game after all, just standing in a different position known as the sideline, where the view was a little different.

I learned the importance of setting boundaries. I took a personal inventory and prayerfully and carefully saw who and what I was capable of allowing into my circle. I learned that reviewing my circle of acquaintances was necessary for my growth. How did I feel when that person left my presence? Did their conversation bring any peace to my soul? Are they here to grieve me or celebrate me? How did I feel about myself? Is he or she connected to my destiny? What is the purpose of their existence in my life? More importantly, did God send them? And so forth and so on. This was how I set boundaries; I had to if I was going to heal properly.

Although you couldn't pay me to believe some folk who started this journey with me would not remain with me to the conclusion of the matter. Life changes with time. Forgiveness brought healing. Now, I can be in the presence of those who hurt me having no need to repay their indignity. My heart no longer beats so fast I can't breathe, the palms of my hands no longer sweat, no dry mouth, no headache, blood pressure is normal; nothing but peace, and **that,** my friend is indescribable!

Lee Jenkins, Darryl Fitzgerald, and Craig Minor: *The 'Brothas'*

Lee and I have been friends for nearly twenty-plus years. We have some stories that would make you laugh and cry! Hanging out with Cynthia and me in our apartment, (we had to feed the brother, cause he was what? *Broke*!) When neither one of us had two quarters to rub together; we always dreamed about our destinies. Lee encouraged me to pursue my dreams with confidence. He once told me, "Girl, you're a life-changer."

Even though Lee's a great friend and brother, I had to revoke his 'match-making license' – he introduced me to my ex-husband! (You blew it, dude!) Our relationship has been proven in its purity. Lee is not selfish with his wisdom and financial insight, as a matter of fact I can call him for advice and he freely gives it.

He will fight for and with me to the end. Today he's a busy, successful wealth advisor, speaker and author, with two incredible must reads; *Taking Care of Business* and *What to Do When Your Money is Funny*. Yet, he's never too busy to holla' at his girl! Thanks for being there. I'm so very proud to call you friend!

Words from Lee:
To say that Debra Winans has been a great friend of mine for well over twenty-years is an understatement. She has been more than a friend; she has been FAMILY. Debra has been like a sister to me in every sense of the word.

We met in our early twenties when we were both trying to figure out what God had called us to do. We had no money and no job. To be honest with you, we were rather pitiful! However, we did have a vision for our lives and we held on to that vision as if our lives depended on it, because it did. We both knew that with God all things were possible.

God used Debra's friendship in my life to encourage me to never give up. No matter how bad things were looking for me at that time, Debra was always there with a smile on her face to tell me I could do it. She lived out Proverbs 17:17 in my life, "A friend loves at all times, and a brother [or sister] is born for adversity."

As God has blessed me, I often reflect back on those early days of my friendship with Debra. God used her to keep me on track towards His ultimate calling for my life. For that, I am forever grateful to her.

Darryl is my buffer. He's my voice of truth. Darryl kept me from going too far left in my anger. He would not let me shut down; he kept me talking yet helped me to focus and balance. If I was headed in the "going there" direction, he would give me the look only Darryl Fitzgerald could give! He's a bottom-line person, cut-to-the- chase man, but a great encourager and listener. I must add even though I'm older than he, he *really thinks he's my big brother*! I know Darryl will be there for me come rain or shine. A diligent man of God, he prays and covers my entire household. He's married to my girl Steph, which is no wonder they make such a great team! Thank you for being one upon whom I can continue to lean.

Words from Darryl:
If you are fortunate you will have a few friends in this world. I mean people who see the best and the worst of you and still love, not judge

you. That is a friend. Proverbs 17:17 says, "A friend loves at all times." Proverbs 27:6 says, "Wounds from a friend can be trusted." A true friend knows how to delicately practice both sides of friendship and Debbie can do both. I call this type of person 'a gentle warrior.'

I remember when my wife and I got married over fifteen years ago we struggled as a young couple in the first few years trying to adjust to being married. Not only did Deb encourage us in our struggle but she did not condemn us either. She simply loved us but she also told us the truth! It is good to have people you can be ***real*** *with and not* ***religious****. Now, the good news about our friendship is Debbie knows love and friendship works both ways. If I do not agree with something she says or does, she allows me to speak the truth to her in love. She often complains that I am hard on her because I* <u>*act*</u> *like her big brother. That is because she gives me the freedom to be so.*

As I stated earlier, you are fortunate if you have a few friends in this world, I can truly say Deb has been one to my wife, family and myself as well. She has always been an encouragement to us in the best of times and the worst of times.

Craig and I were always good friends but we became closer in the last few years. Craig is one of the most generous people I know. We could sit and talk for hours. He would call at least five times a day, singing some off-color song thinking he's Nat King Cole or Luther Vandross!

Patiently allowing me to flow in and out of my emotions, he would make me laugh so hard tears would run down my face. His wit and strong presence put my mind at ease. When I would try to hibernate within, Craig would come by and take me to one of *his* favorite spots to eat, whether I liked it or not! He couldn't stand to see me cry, so he would make me laugh!

To this present day, Craig reminds me I am a gift, not a prize, that whoever receives me as a wife will be a blessed man. But, he would also tell me, not before he takes that man to his 'interrogation room' to check him out! He is truly my brother, my brother for life!

(During the editing of this book, Craig passed away. I'm sure going to miss him. I loved him so much; he was my dear friend and close brother. I did have the opportunity to read to Craig what I wrote of him and our friendship. As his eyes filled with tears, I believe it was the first time I saw him speechless. The earth will miss this remarkable man.)

Although I have five natural brothers, these three men are my brothers as well. They are very protective of me and will cut you if you mess with me! Each one is very special in his own right, but their common thread is strength. I knew they would bear me up when my strength failed.

They heard me, and they responded; not only to and for me, but my children as well. School visits, showing up to "uncle" the kids was God-sent. It seemed when I was in the middle of one of my many melt downs, one of these extraordinary men would ring my door bell!

We all shared innumerable days of laughter! Oh, don't think for a moment they didn't get on my nerves trying to run my house and theirs! But one thing is for sure I wouldn't trade them for anything in this world. I don't know who's worse, my five brothers or these three. Either way, I am sincerely grateful I have them all.

Lisa Booker: *The Faithful*

Lisa has an unselfish nature. No matter what state I have seen her in she never fails to wear a sweet smile. Her life seems to produce healing. Lisa thrives by assisting people, helping them to walk in their purpose. She literally and gently guides people through their oftentimes challenging financial set-backs.

Lisa is a successful real estate loan officer and financial preparedness instructor. Even though her schedule is hectic, her family always comes first. Our daughters have been best friends since kindergarten; she loves my children like her own.

This woman is also a source of consistent strength and encouragement to me. She too, thinks I can do anything but fail. She's been a tremendous supporter and friend. Although she's old school, I enjoy watching her transition into a 21st century woman! (You better go, Girl!) Our conversations are rich and filled with possibilities to become better mothers, women, and friends. Lisa's friendship is priceless, one I will always cherish. You are indeed a phenomenal woman, Mz. Lisa!

Words from Lisa:
God has His best things for the few who dare to stand the test! My heart rejoices in Debra, as she's accomplished this milestone in her life. I knew that her talents and abilities would someday bless others. I am so proud of her accomplishments, and I know that God is well pleased! Debra inspires me to do my best and reach my goals. I am grateful to have a friend that challenges me to reach beyond the norm! I am so honored to call her friend!

Let me digress for a moment. *The Lord of the Rings* included six other men. They too had an assignment in assisting Frodo. Each man understood their particular task, each one moving toward the same goal. Should one measure or judge the significance of his or her assignment by comparing it to another? It is not wise to do so. (See 2 Cor. 10:12)

The complexity of that path is more tolerable to trail when you know someone greater than yourself is walking alongside you.

The vastly incredible people in my life accepted their assignment regarding me and it kept me above ground. Every person is significant in your life, whether good, bad or indifferent, temporary or permanent. There is an original intent for our lives. We are not some kind of cosmic accident. Whether you believe it or not it's still true. Life's mishaps are what shape us, and strengthen us. Friendships are what we hold fast to. But trust and faith in God is what sustains and directs us. He is **the only One** who knows how the stories of our lives begin and end.

He knows, even in the midst of our often bad choices, what needs to be kept, erased, or blended into the tapestry of our lives. Knowing that God was fully aware of every intricate detail of my journey gave me assurance that *I am not in control*, **<u>He is!</u> God is Sovereign...period!**

> *Giving up my* ***right*** *to prove someone wrong was the battle I fought to hold on to...*

As the men of *The Lord of the Rings* each focused on their designated and complex paths, so must we fiercely maintain our focus on the path we have been given. The complexity of that path is more tolerable to trail when you know someone greater than yourself is walking alongside you. Some people do not have the insight or the character to be to you what you have been to them. They may be incapable of giving you what you need. Or perhaps it was purposely withheld for whatever the reason. Regrettably, the greatest moments and opportunities of being a friend can be missed in those instances.

Some believe that by deliberately withholding a possible need or opportunity from you, when it is within their power to give it, that the need or opportunity will not be granted. That is far from the truth. The truth is that they will entirely miss the pleasure of reaping the benefit of being blessed in countless ways from countless directions by supplying what you seek. Besides, it is biblically incorrect to do so! (Prov. 29:21 KJV and NLT)

So as with every office of Solomon's great administration came great responsibility. The title of 'friend' also carries great accountability. With every level of friendship there is a level of transparency. Can we take responsibility for the part we played in the relationships that have gone sour? Some relationships are toxic. Let them go. As my sister-in-love Veronica says, one must decide to "grow with or go on." A close inventory of our relationships is vital, healthy, and necessary.

My expecting a return on some friendship investments was not always realistic. My acceptance of the truth of its status was a hard slap in the face. Anytime there is a breach in relationship, it's painful. As much as I wanted to fix this, I could not. Giving up my **right** to prove someone wrong was the battle I fought to hold on to, but I soon came to realize that people do whatever they choose to do. Although it hurt deeply, I fought hard to maintain my ability to love and to remain a friend.

The place I frequent called *Still*, (that I mentioned in the first chapter) is my place that reminds me how grateful to God I am for not allowing me to drown in myself. He did not allow me to self-destruct. This safe place is not only when I was hurting, but a place where I receive peace daily. There will always be something or someone that reminds you how much you need the Lord every single day, in every single area of your life.

Pam Green: The Protector;
Elayne C. Calhoun: The Truth-Bearer;
Sylvia Reid: The Anchor

Pam and I were childhood friends. Our families knew each other since our teenage days. She is another long distance relationship, but we've walked down the road of uncertainty many a day. We laugh at all the madness we both have gone through. But we also can't help but cry reflecting how far we've come and how much we've grown. With children of our own, we are determined to teach, model and train them to be all they desire to be and not carry unnecessary baggage into any relationship - something she and I are still learning today.

The position of 'baby-sisters' can sometime blind our siblings from accepting that we are now adult women and mothers. It is true they've seen us suffer, yet time has forced them to admit God has carried us through it all. It's his time to proudly admit we are stronger than realized. Pam is my long time friend and sister. Look at us now girl. We made it through and we're still cute!

Words from Pam:
Debra is my longest standing friend – almost 30 years. I first met Debra Johnson when we were both teenagers 17 or 18-years-old. I

was traveling with my family the summer of 1980 on an evangelistic outreach to several cities. Atlanta was one of the ministry stops we had on the schedule that year. My oldest brother knew the hosting family from previous years of ministry with another group. He was invited back and that time, he brought us, his family and a few friends for that time of ministry. Debbie and I met and hit if off immediately. Maybe because we were both, "baby sisters" of preachers; we were both a part of families drenched and trained in ministry both in singing and in the Word; we had so very much in common. For a period of time, we lost contact with each other, but we were physically rejoined around 1986. At that time, she had just gotten married and I was about to be married. We never lost contact again.

We're both all grown up now! We both have families of our own. We have both since the time of our meeting gone through a lot together. We have cried together, laughed together, prayed together, encouraged one another and pushed each other to excellence. I've watched her maneuver her way through some rocky and very hard, sometimes lonely places, even when the odds were against her. She truly has the love of God in her and she gives unselfishly. She is the one who showed me how to love myself; how to take care of me; how to pick myself back up even after a devastating life-altering event in my life. Debra was there literally, physically, emotionally, spiritually and financially. She was always there, loyal and very strong. Debbie is endeared to my entire family. My children affectionately call her 'Auntie Debbie.' I affectionately call her my sister and my friend.

Elayne is my 'Mr. Spock' friend! She's the logical one. She will analyze the matter until there is absolutely nothing else to dissect! Elayne is very honest. She's a no-holds-barred sister. Elayne is a truth-bearer. If you don't want to know the truth, DO NOT, I repeat, DO NOT ask Elayne! What's funny about her is, as straight forward as she is, she's the biggest crybaby you ever want to meet! Have you ever had someone tell you off and cry at the same time? And she DOES NOT raise her voice!

Cool, calm, and collected, that's my girl, Elayne Calcote Calhoun! I love this woman. She is a remarkable person, she helped me to come face to face with areas I did not feel was important to address at the time but she saw the potential of my destruction if I didn't. Pressing me softly, I didn't realize how much she carried me through until I reached the other side. With the most beautiful smile ever, she softly added, "See, you made it, that wasn't so bad!" Elayne, you were right again!

Words from Elayne:
'Dee,' I affectionately call her; we have known each other for quite some time. We have laughed until we cried and even cried until we laughed. Her infectious smile and warm, kind spirit are just a few things I love most about her. Dee's amazing faith and strength in God has been a model for us ALL!

Thinking back to the first time we met, I can't help remembering how we sized each other up, checking each other out from head to toe a few times! We smiled cordially and nothing else was said for a long time. It always makes me laugh out loud when I reminisce about our first encounter.

Little did I know that she would be one of the most caring, dependable, generous, and protective friends that I have. Some people live their lives without a true friend. I have been blessed by God to have a friend like Dee in my life. She has been there for me many times with her spirit-filled words of encouragement.

I remember we were at her home in Dallas, Texas sitting around in our pajamas catching up on old times. She shared her recent frustrating experiences, and although she was in tears while telling me the story, we began to laugh so hard I literally fell off the side of the bed! Girl, thank you for being you! Thanks for loving me just like I am and not requiring me to change a thing! Always here for you Dee!

Sylvia is my California sister. Always full of life, Sylvia and I think so much alike, it's a little scary. Her mother, Lady Pearl and my mother could have passed for twin sisters. Although we have known each other for only a few years, we share a deep sisterhood. We have each other's backs. We are protective of each other's hearts, minds and ministries. Finishing one another's sentences, we chuckle at the devices people use to sabotage friendships, and determine it will not work on us. Pearls of wisdom shared through Sylvia, have truly blessed my life. She is truly one of a kind. We acknowledge and celebrate the princess in each other, while we don't quite understand why others don't! Oh well, it is what it is… Smooches Girlfriend!

Words from Sylvia:
Debra Winans is responsible for me not being in jail today! (Cause there have been times I was ready to hurt somebody…BAD— No— For real!). Sorry, I was having a flashback! Having Debra as a friend means I have wisdom, guidance, encouragement, comfort and sanctuary. In other words, I have the love of Christ manifest in human form. Our friendship is not dictated by time or space but by mutual concern, appreciation and love.

Whoever gets me gets her – we are a package deal! Princesses united for a better world!

Richard Johnson: The Tower; Veronica Johnson: The Pillar

Veronica and I were friends long before she married my brother Richard. She's a big sister to me. I always knew I could trust her. I was ecstatic when they married, because our relationship became even closer. We have enjoyed our friendship for over twenty-plus years.

Veronica is a type of security blanket, safe, comfortable and warm. No matter how old the relationship, Veronica is my solace. I find comfort in her still. She is precious. She has carried me in prayer and cried with me through sorrows. She rejoices with me and speaks truth without reservation. She too has been with me in different facets of my life, always there to encourage and cheer me on. She reminds me that God's purpose and plan for my life is awesome; and she warns me that I better not forget her when I come into my 'kingdom.' Veronica, you are one of a kind!

Words from Veronica:
Debbie was my friend long before I married her brother and became her "Sister-in-Love." We have walked together through many seasons of

life. Sometimes crying, praying, laughing, celebrating, rejoicing and encouraging each other. I know that God really loves me to have Deb as my "Sister-friend."

As she walked through a season of great trials, I began to question God. "How long does she have to go through this? When will You vindicate her and shut the mouth of her enemies? Enough is enough Lord! Please hurry up! I didn't realize that God was doing a marvelous thing in her life. He was building character and integrity within her to protect the great anointing she was carrying. By the way, one of her greatest anointings is to be a true friend-unconditionally. She taught me how to go through a trial and not render 'evil for evil.' Time after time, I saw God hold her peace and close her mouth. He didn't want her speaking harmful words that could destroy her future testimony.

I am so thankful for this new season of her life. It is a season of gracious favor and tremendous increase. Goodness and Mercy are her familiar friends. God will force her enemy to watch Him prepare a table of great blessings for her. Deb, remember, No one can change God's mind about you. He is madly in love with you!

Richard is my natural brother. He is the second to the oldest son. This is the brother who taught me how to braid my hair and cook spaghetti. This brother carved out "us" time. This is the brother who gave me my middle name, and I am still his baby. This brother ran all my little boyfriends away! He's also the brother that told me I was beautiful. One Easter morning, when I was a little girl our Mom would dress me in very girly apparel - frills, white tights and white lacy gloves. My hair arranged in Shirley Temple Curls which was the style of the day. I would make my grand entrance into the living room. Mom would stand me up on the piano bench as my brothers 'oohed and aahed' with applause.

Richard's face is the one I remember seeing as he took my hand to slowly twirl me around like a jewel box ballerina. He was always proud of me. To this present day, my brother is as gentle with me as he was when I stood on that piano bench.

I can share it all with Richard, my confidant. He has walked with me through each sequel of my life and remained free of judgment and criticism. Speaking truth firmly, lovingly and openly has never been his weakness. Richard possesses character that is second to none.

Richard, loyal sometimes to a fault but you can't beat knowing *this* man. Although he tells the worst jokes you ever heard! By the way, only his kids and niece, Miya, thinks his jokes are the best. My brother is a mans-man who is admired and respected by many. With everything within me Richard, I honor you. Undisputedly, You...Are...My...Hero!

Words from Richard:
Debra, better known as 'Baby' is my youngest sister who has a great ability to say what is difficult...the unspoken thing, the painful thing, things that need to be said. As you read her story, you'll find yourself on a journey, an adventure into your own story. Debra is so much more than my youngest sister. Hot or cold, light or dark, up or down, (the extremes were the same tn Deb's and my relationship), you were there. The love in our hearts bolstered us, no matter what...our decision was made a long time ago, to love.

If my memory serves me well, having to go without; there you were. Enduring turbulent times, enjoying good success, there you were. And when I said yes to my wife and when my children were born, there you were, and still, here you are, being you like no other. Only God could construct a YOU, Baby, and to Him I am grateful.

I look forward to all our tomorrows. Knowing that you'll be in our lives. Knowing you'll be in my life still brings great joy. Debra, words do fail: but I cannot let it go unsaid...Thank you. I love you.

There it is – my friendship journey. These jewels showed me I was not intended to always stand alone. Each one genuinely cared about and believed in me. Destiny is not just about where you're going but who God has assigned to help get you there. For me, these are the "Samwise Gamgees" of my life. With an overwhelmed heart of love and honor, I salute you all – I know you know this but I want the whole world to know it as well!

I learned the quantity assigned to your camp is not as important as the quality. So, I can safely say, c'*est la vie* to those persons who chose not to stay around. Perhaps they weren't supposed to. Jesus Himself walked with the seventy-two, then the twelve and then the three. Truly there is a time and season for all things. I couldn't have asked for a better group of friends and family. They are indeed the crème de la crème.

Destiny is not
just about where you're going
but who God has assigned
to help get you there.

Describe the essence of friendship to you.

Write a prayer of thanksgiving for your friendships.

JOURNEY EIGHT

Perception is Everything!

When I turned the big 4-0, I had a wonderful birthday bash. It was fab-u-lous; truly *An Affair to Remember!* The invitations were beautifully designed by my friend, Veronica Hawbaker of Vee Design. The theme "*Fit, Fine, and Fabulous at Forty!*" spoke of an event unlike any other, and requested the presence of friends and family to join me for this illustrious milestone.

The invitation itself was a conversation piece – a keepsake of its own. I had worked hard to lose over fifty-pounds, so I felt beautiful and sexy as I posed in the studio of professional photographer Michael Gomez. In one shot, I was 'cheesing' holding up four fingers and a zero. In another shot, I wore a black cat suit with a bejeweled hip-belt and blew kisses at the camera. And in another shot, I was draped in sheer elegance. The highlight for this photo shoot for me was the joy of including my two beautiful babies. My celebration began with this shoot. Typically photo shoots are not much fun, but I had a ball that day. Oh yeah, I was fit, fine, and fabulous at forty!

My birthday outfit was the bomb! I wore an iridescent purple and teal blue long-fitted dress that had spaghetti straps and three-quarter length sleeves. My popped-collar coat that brushed the floor put the "exclamation mark" on my ensemble. I wore handcrafted clear-stoned necklace and earrings and sling-back high heeled shoes that were dyed to match my dress. My make-up and hair were laid OUT!

My fairy-tale evening was held at the Hilton Suites Hotel in downtown Nashville, the newest and most elegant hotel in the city. The ballroom was transformed into sophisticated opulence by my friend Regenia Knight. Each table was exquisitely dressed with its own personality of purple, gold, and silver accoutrements.

I was honored with celebrities, politicians, business people, religious leaders, recording artists, professional athletes, friends, family and even a few former in-laws. It seemed everyone was having the best time. Three-hundred plus guests awaited my birthday entrance. My godfather, Pastor Kennith Barrington captured the audience's attention with a special presentation on the essence of forty. His silky-smooth baritone voice puts you in mind of James Earl Jones.

My entrance was choreographed by multi-talented Denise Marcia. As the soundtrack from the motion picture, *The First Knight* struck, I felt like a queen! The mahogany double doors were opened and I stepped into this beautiful room where the excitement was booming with anticipation. This was truly a monumental moment for me.

All five of my brothers, looked quite handsome, if I say so myself! They were dressed in black tuxedos, posted at each corner of the dance floor. I entered the room with the grandeur of Jackie Kennedy Onasis. Swept up in the whirlwind of fantasy come to reality, I seemed to glide to my youngest brother for the first dance. As the enchantment of the music continued, that brother waltzed me to the next oldest. The transfer continued until my hand was placed in the hand of my oldest brother, Flynn who was awaiting me in the center of the floor. Each partner signified my crossing over from one dimension of life to another successfully. I curtsied to each one with gratitude, for this was their celebration as well as mine.

The night for me, would not have been complete without a surprise presentation to my special friends. My desire was to give each one something of significance, so I wrote them a letter about our friendship printed on beautiful paper rolled in a scroll. It was a tear-jerking night to say the least; it meant the world to me to bless them. What a beautiful celebration of dancing, singing, dining, mingling, and sharing; a night I shall always cherish.

Something happened to my psyche at forty, my perspective regarding life was magnified. My confidence became energized. The view seemed simpler and clearer. I became more serious and exact regarding my life decisions. My tolerance for foolishness shortened. I was intensely more focused. The scales began to peel from my eyes, causing me to see the bigger picture of my purpose.

Speaking of sight, two weeks before my party, I went for an eye examination. Typically, I wore stylish non-prescription reading glasses from Stein Mart and T.J. Maxx. In denial of needing prescription glasses, this would suffice for now, I thought. I wasn't aware I was weakening my sight by wearing the non-prescription glasses. My eyes-glasses now required medication.

As the optometrist continued the eye examination, I was wondering why the letters on the chart appeared so small! After the examination, we chit-chatted for a moment and I shared with him how I used to read for hours in poor lighting. I ignored the frequent headaches, chucking it off to the fact I might have been tired. He asked a few pertinent questions relating to my occupation, family history, my last eye exam, my age and so forth. When I told him my age, I was compelled to share the enveloping event of my upcoming fortieth birthday party. He patronized me saying he could see why I was excited, since he did not think I was a day over 30! (Cool points for the doc!)

But then he knocked the wind out of my sails when he gave me shocking news! He said, "*Even though you don't look a day over 30, according to the results of your eye exam your sight is that of a 45-year-old!*" WHAT? My hearing must be fading too! To add insult to injury, he said I needed to put away the stylish non-prescription glasses because he was writing a *prescription* for reading glasses and contacts. Oh my! I couldn't believe what I was hearing. The fact is my sight was not what it used to be. The truth is I had better get that prescription filled in order to have my vision sharpened!

The word 'optometry' is derived from the word opt; it means 'vision or see.' I know people who have 20/20 vision or better. Some are far-sighted, near-sighted or have what is called astigmatism, which is about the way light is reflecting in the eye. It is difficult for the light to reach the part of the eye that sees clearly. It's a misalignment of the eye's ability to see light. In addition to astigmatism, a person could develop glaucoma, which is pressure building in the eye and if not corrected, could lead to blindness.

Throughout my journey I've been misaligned. We are creatures of habit. Change is not comfortable and at times, even a little frightening. There were moments I bucked against this process of changing how I saw myself due to many misfortunes of life. Sometimes if people put you down long enough, the 'bad stuff' is easier to believe (You ever notice that?). Dr. Myles Munroe said it this way: "The lie has become so popular that the truth appears to be an imposter." However, when light or "revelation" presents itself, it awakens something on the inside of you. Light oftentimes begins to challenge your ability to handle or apply truth correctly. If I focused on what I did or did not say or do right, I would remain in a constant state of total misalignment and confusion which eventually would lead to blindness, or fragmented dreams.

Dr. Myles Munroe said it this way: "The lie has become so popular that the truth appears to be an imposter."

You know, sometimes we give people too much power. We allow them to think their word is law or that my life, your life will move forward or backward upon their spoken word...**WRONG!**

When I speak of light and revelation, I'm speaking specifically of what God has to say about you and your future. What truly matters is what He says about who you are and the purpose for which you were placed on this earth. Besides, He's the owner of all time and space anyway. What God says is right always, adds life, bears truth and brings revelation to the whole man – spirit, soul and body.

We are faced with the illumination of our perspective, only to mask ourselves in deception, settling for the state of blindness. Therefore, we remain in our astigmatic state rather than making a change in order to live life purposefully. Life is strategically designed – it is chess, not checkers.

We all come face-to-face with what and how we see ourselves, our purpose and our destiny. The longer you delay or ignore your "life-exam," the more difficult it becomes; the magnifying glasses are of no effect. Oh, I was stunning the night of my party, but let me tell you, when it came time for me to read my presentations, I had to borrow my brother's prescription glasses because I was too cute to get my prescription filled!

What God says
is right always,
adds life,
bears truth and
brings revelation
to the whole man –
spirit, soul and body.

How you posture yourself contributes to your perception. The Majestic Beach Towers has 22 floors. The ocean view side of the condos has a clear view, so no matter what floor you are on, you can see the ocean. However, the higher the floor, the more brilliant and vast the view! A shift in your position broadens how well and how far you "see." Do not sell yourself short; the view of your future is breathtaking. Granted, life may have thrown you a few curve balls, but I challenge you to no longer be afraid to go back and pull out those dormant dreams.

It wasn't too long ago you stored away your dream journals; it wasn't too long ago you saw yourself prosperous and free to "be" who you truly are. Today, I hope to position you for the penthouse view! Open your eyes, my friend and see as far as your mind's eye can see. You've been given permission to dream again. Embrace your destiny as you move full throttle into greatness.

Open your eyes,
my friend and see
as far as your mind's
eye can see. You've
been given permission
to dream again.
Embrace your destiny
as you move full
throttle into greatness.

I conclude this chapter with a reflection from the movie *The Lion King:*

> *Simba heard his father Mufasa call to him from the billow of clouds. "Simba, you have forgotten me." Simba replies, "No, how could I?" Mufasa continues, "You*

> *have forgotten who you are and so forgotten me. Look inside yourself Simba, you are more than what you have become, you must take your place in the Circle of Life." Simba asks, "How can I go back? I'm not who I used to be." Mufasa states, "Remember who you are, you are my son and the one true king. Remember who you are...Remember...Remember!"*

The wind is indeed changing. Sometimes we need a monkey to club us cover the head to remind us we can *run* from our past or *learn* from it! Break the silence of your despair and pain as you remember who you are. *You are the King's kid! Remember... Remember!*

How do you perceive yourself? Go deeper than 'cute,' or 'plump,' or 'I have ugly feet ugly,' etc. Be real and be healed. Write about your character and your flaws.

*Write down areas **you** must change in order to see yourself from the Penthouse view!*

JOURNEY NINE

The Best Is Yet To Come

Of course, *The Lion King* is a fictional story, but it contains many applicable truths. The sovereignty of God is not fictional; it's the real deal and gauge for life. According to Hebrews 13:5-6, ***He** will **never leave you** neither forsake you; He will be with you until the **end** of **time**, [or the end of yourself].* (Emphasis and brackets my own.)

The original intent of our lives is ***His*** plan spoken before the foundation of the earth. When you decide it is not enough to know of Him, and you truly come to know Him for yourself, you will experience life and life more abundantly. I'm not naïve to think that I have or am experiencing the abundant life to its fullest to date. Yet and still, I am constantly pursuing the journey to greatness because I am in pursuit of ***Him*** daily. He chose my journey and those with whom I must share that journey, as well as those who will be blessed because of it. With each waking day, I look forward to every promise, every dream, and every manifestation of the joy of being in complete wholeness.

Joseph was sold into slavery by his brothers. Later he was falsely accused by a woman and served prison time. He was forgotten and alone. Through the sovereignty of God, Joseph was appointed governor. He was placed in a position to assist the very brothers who betrayed him. (See Gen. 44-45)

Esther is another example. An orphan who was raised by her uncle; she went from obscurity to royalty, becoming the most powerful queen ever; she was born 'for such a time as this.' (See the Book of Esther)

Then there's another young girl who, like Esther, lost both parents and was raised by a relative. She too was chosen to serve kings and priests. Her human misfortunes and calamities were designed by one to destroy her, and they almost did, so it seemed.

But she was a rare, exquisite "*Divine Design*." Created by the One who knew the purpose for which she was created and knew what was needed to bring her into that purpose. She is now a businesswoman, author and corporate consultant, who strategizes for many of the nation's leading organizations.

My commitment to Christ is what kept me inhaling and exhaling each second of the day.

I am this woman and my story is not over. I have yet to reach the zenith of my life. But like Esther, I have found myself in the presence of greatness, speaking on behalf of those who could not speak for themselves. Yet with each faith-filled vertical leap, I remain steadfast, confident, well-balanced and poised as a queen, assured of the purpose of my existence.

My special place I call ***Still*** is found solely in my Lord and Savior Jesus Christ. Stillness was not always a welcomed place for me because it required discipline of my entire being. I found a place of quiet isolation and yet it was also place of turmoil and complexity.

Like Jacob, I wrestled with my old nature and uncertain future until I came face-to-face with the One I loved and to whom I was most committed. My commitment to Christ was greater than my pain and any latent desires to defend myself or retaliate against those who wounded me. My commitment to Christ is what kept me inhaling and exhaling each second of the day. No doubt my pain was great; nevertheless, my love and my commitment were greater.

No doubt my pain was great; nevertheless, my love and my commitment were greater.

The Scripture says it clearly in Philippians 3:10 (KJV), "*That I may **know him** in the power of his resurrection and the **fellowship of his sufferings**....*" *Verse 13-14, "Brethren I do not count myself to have apprehended; but one thing I do **forgetting** those things which are **behind** and **reaching forward** to those things which are **ahead**, I* *press toward the goal for the prize of the* ***upward call*** *of God* ***in*** *Christ Jesus."* (Emphasis mine.)

My pastor made a statement at a funeral that was so powerful to me. He said, "*...pain is a gift nobody wants, but it's the gift Christ Jesus gave freely.*"

The Lord Jesus Christ, He is my Protector, my Provider, my Shelter, my forever Friend. I owe Him my life, He is my, well...**Everything!** I trust Him even when I can't trace Him. I count it an honor that He entrusted me with this journey and journeys I have yet to trod. I came to realize I could attempt to change my mind about many things, but I **could not** change my destiny. He will forever have the final word. And I'm OK with that!

I believe God thoroughly enjoys doing the preposterous. I can imagine it is quite exhilarating and delightful to Him turning weaknesses into strengths, fears into faith, lack into supply, that which has been marred into perfection. This sounds like we are all candidates for the Master's use!

I believe God thoroughly enjoys doing the preposterous. I can imagine it is quite exhilarating and delightful to Him turning weaknesses into strengths, fears into faith, lack into supply, that which has been marred into perfection. This sounds like we are all candidates for the Master's use!

You are not alone – and you are not delusional. Life doesn't wait on the wounded it keeps moving! Get back in the saddle, set your face like flint, and ride into the sunset. Or pull out your compact mirror, look at your beautiful self, and say emphatically, "*My best days are ahead of me, no doubt.*"

Look forward to being in love again; I do! Look forward to undiscovered territory; I am! Life may have taken its best shot, knocked you down more than once, but you have found a way to get back up, time and time again. We may have been stuck between *if* and *when*, but time and purpose ceaselessly brings us through.

My friend Dr. Elaine Waller says, "*There are times when things look as if we've lost our dreams, and our significance was in the fact that we oftentimes have knowledge yet lack wisdom. We haven't gone through enough experience to understand that God will allow the enemy to rock our world. God will make you significant in the earth to affect others for His glory. Yet, between the dream and the fulfillment is the drama.*"

The wisdom gained from our experiences was not merely for us alone, but there are men and women who need guidance out of a sea of despair and hopelessness. Who better to lead them out than you? Resist the urge to ask, 'Why me?' and ask rather, 'Why not me?'

God will make you significant in the earth to affect others for His glory. Yet, between the dream and the fulfillment is the drama."

Your audience awaits you. No more blending in. You were born to stand out! Why do bad things happen to good people in life? That's a valid question, but unimportant to the matter at hand, which is Greatness. It calls you from the pillar of the cloud and from the heavens above, shouting your name, "Wake up! Get up! Move forward! Don't retreat from the battle! To stay is bitter, to move forward is better!"

You are the messenger who carries the message of life and hope. Your life, my life might be the only book some people will ever read. What's written on your pages? What will you deposit? Life or death? Peace or despair? Truth or deception? How will your life impact others? Will you offer joy or sorrow? Freedom or bondage?

As the general in the movie, *The Gladiator* says, "*What we do in life echoes in eternity.*" I am determined to be a better whole person in every area of my life. I pledge to be the mother my children will respect, honor, and model. My mission in life is to see men and women healed from the inside out and to operate in the carte blanche favor and destiny of God!

As for you with a scarlet-lettered past, a tattered-and-torn heart, you too, are right on time's schedule and targeted to experience an abundant life full of blessing far beyond your imagination. But the caveat is this...it's really up to you! So, what are you waiting for? Is there life during your wilderness journey? Absolutely! Will the journey of life continue? You better believe it. I leave you with the reminder that there is hope at the end of the journey, for Jeremiah 29:11 declares, "*I know the thoughts and plans that I have for you, says the Lord, thoughts and plans for welfare and peace and not for evil, to give you hope in your final outcome.*" (Amplified version)

> *"Wake up!*
> *Get up!*
> *Move forward!*
> *Don't retreat*
> *from the battle!*
> *To stay is bitter,*
> *to move forward*
> *is better!"*

The Lord is the only reason I can write this book, face my foes, and fulfill my dreams. Why? Long before I was a thought in my parents' hearts, my life was already established on the pages of eternity. And so was yours.

You've had some questions about today's realities,
And so many feelings, different feelings about tomorrow's uncertainties.
These same questions have been answered for me,
And I am resting in the promise of what my eyes have yet to see.
If you'll believe in His goodness, believe in His love,
The best of life is waiting for you.
Wouldn't you like to know what the future has in store?
What God has chosen for you behind tomorrow's door?
Can you imagine all of His promises to you?
No more reaction. No retraction. Everything He said is true.
If you believe in His goodness, and believe in His love,
The best in life is waiting for you.
Just keep on doing the things He told you,
believing the things He said,
You won't walk in darkness and you'll never be afraid.

Hold on to those promises the Lord has given you.
The best in life is waiting –
The very best in life is waiting for you.

So stop interpreting your life by your circumstance. Perpetual pain is designed to destroy you, your vision, and your dreams. But right in the middle of it all, let *Perpetual Praise* conquer and prevail! I plead with you to deal with the pain, release your fears and embrace your destiny as you journey on your road to wholeness and peace. Now is the time to make *your* distinct mark in the earth!

What is in your life that you think you cannot chunge?

*If fear **were not** an issue in your life, what would you accomplish?*

JOURNEY TEN

The Lily and You!

If I were asked to pinpoint the major turning points in my life, I would have to say it began one Sunday morning on Mother's Day when Dr. Elaine Waller preached one of the most awesome messages I ever heard.

As I absorbed that message, I now had insight into the place I formally referred to as 'bewilderment.' To my amazement, it wasn't bewilderment at all. Now replete with understanding, I learned this place was called "A Field of Lilies." I clung to every word that proceeded from her mouth. My ears were fine-tuned, to what my spirit recognized as truth and precise clarity; finally, a sketched picture that I could now identify.

With all my heart, I sincerely pray that what you read and earnestly digest in the final chapter of this book will revolutionize your very being. A parable is clearly crafted before you. Take heart dear one, help is not on the way, it is here! You are not going crazy; you are a lily blossoming in this field called Life!

Allow me to recap that message for you. The lily only grows in the valley. The lily doesn't look like other flowers. The cow or calla lilies are grown in dry, hard, parched, and cold places where the temperature shifts back and forth. The flower won't bud if the temperature stays the same; it needs extreme climate in order to grow! Sounds familiar?

The leaves protect the flower, and cover it until the bud is full grown. The fragrance of the lily is in the bud. From the bud comes 192 perfumes, Giorgio Armani gets all its origin from the lily as well as Elizabeth Taylor's *White Diamonds* and *Passion*, to name a few scents. The lily's broad leaves, white bell shaped flowers, requires an extreme shift in temperature. It will not grow in consistent temperature, if the lily is over-watered, its leaves will not spring up high enough to sustain the length of the flower. It does not have a designated season when it springs up. Only when the pendulum of extreme heat or extreme cold swing its way does the aromatic bud bloom. Isn't it interesting that as we traverse life's adversities that we see the depth of what we are made of? It is the sway of life's pendulum that causes our true self to blossom.

> *How often have you seen people quit, or throw in the towel because they could not handle the rocky places of their lives any longer? You, however, were able to bloom where you were planted.*

The roots of the lily are so strong they often require a rocky, dry, uncultivated ground in which to grow. God uses the uncultivated extremes of our lives to make us grow. How often have you seen people quit, or throw in the towel because they could not handle the rocky places of their lives any longer? You, however, were able to bloom where you were planted.

You have grown through the heat and cold of your adversities. Your roots of convictions and principles run deep. Everything that seems to entrap, entangle, and confuse you, all the disappointments and perverted mess that comes to destroy you is really what makes you develop!

How extraordinary. When a lily matures, the center of the bell holds beads that are used as a medicine for heart disease. Like the center of the lily's bell, you become the healing agent for someone you don't even know... remember?

There were people who counted us out, finished, done – of no use. But what they didn't count on was that they themselves were used to make us blossom. When you've been purposely over-looked, stepped on; when poisonous words, finger-pointing, and accusations didn't destroy you, your enemies have no other choice than to see your value – up close and personal. "*[The Lord] prepares a table before you in the presence of your enemies...*" (Psalm 23).

The people who have watched you in the valley have to see you exalted. So don't pray God harm your enemy; pray they stay around so they can behold you feasting at the banquet table!

This is not for you to show off; it's for The Lord God to show off in and through you! He expects all the glory from your life. Exalting you is all about Him, you get to be His vessel of honor.

Only lilies grow in the valley. This is not the time to throw in the towel. This is not the time to quit or bail out. Do not reject what God is allowing in your life. Pass the tests and understand the principles. A line from the Disney movie *Mulan* says it well, "*Perhaps the flower that grows in the most adversity is the rarest and most precious flower of all.*"

No wonder lilies are my favorite flower. I now have a greater appreciation for how they grow. The lily is my logo, and my landmark. It will forever remind me that no matter where I'm to flourish and grow, the Lord prepares the soil and conditions of my growth. Since Jesus is the Lily of the Valley, I am not alone.

He expects all the glory from your life. Exalting you is all about Him, you get to be His vessel of honor.

My pastor is not only a great preacher but he's an awesome teacher of the Word of God. This particular teaching was the icing on the cake; it sealed it for me. To share the entire message is a chapter within itself, so I will share a few highlights. This message was entitled "*Getting Through Difficult Seasons*" from (2Corn. 4:7-9; 15-18 *NLT*).

Vs. 7 "*But this precious treasure – this light and power that now shine within us – is held in perishable container, that is, in our weak bodies. So everyone can see that our glorious power is from God and is not our own.*"

Vs. 8 "*We are pressed on every side by troubles, but we are not crushed and broken. We are perplexed, but we don't give up and quit. We are hunted down, but God never abandons us. We get knocked down, but we get up again and keep going.*"

Vs.15 "*All these things are for your benefit. And as God's grace brings more and more people to Christ, there will be great thanksgiving, and God will receive more and more glory.*"

Vs.16 "That is why we never give up. Though our bodies are dying our spirits are being renewed everyday."

Vs.17 "For our present troubles are quite small and won't last very long. Yet they produce for us an immeasurable great glory that will last forever!

But in the midst of our trouble we still should make sound judgments and sound decisions in our perplexity. That is maturity.

Vs.18 "So we don't look at the troubles we can see right now; rather, we look forward to what we have not yet seen. For the troubles we see will soon be over. But the joys to come will last forever"

The truth and nothing but the truth is this, there will always be trouble! As long as you breathe God's air, there will be trouble, guaranteed! But in the midst of our trouble we still should make sound judgments and sound decisions in our perplexity. That is maturity.

Verse 15 says, "*All of these things are for your benefit…*" Basically, all things are designed and channeled in your behalf, your benefit and favor. Here are a few basic points that process you in the tough seasons or while you're growing in the lily field.

- Offer God thanksgiving during your difficult seasons. Nothing in you wants to be thankful in the midst of perplexity and difficulty. Thankfulness will process you <u>out</u> of something; complaining will cause you to go <u>deeper</u> into despair.

- Don't faint or lose heart. Don't let anything or anyone take your God-given courage from you.

- Renew your mind daily. This takes a lot of work, you have to change the way you think. Keep the junk out and the pleasant and uplifting thoughts in! You will never change what you tolerate!

- Afflictions are only for a season *(Thank you Jesus!)*. The germination period is absolutely necessary for a healthy and mature flower!

- Train your mind's eye to see yourself successful. See your process as profitable!

Granted, we are not guaranteed continual mountain-top experiences. But as we go through life's journeys we now recognize the magnificent purpose of each valley. We can get through tough and difficult seasons and become better for it. Boy, this is powerful! Our afflictions are working for us. You know, oftentimes the things we can't see are the very things that establish us. As we journey through life, we are establishing the exceeding weight for our eternity. Listen, it's not our circumstances that we control, but it's our attitude while in the circumstance or trouble. I believe God observes us as we journey through life – how we handle our trouble, or the growth process.

I didn't die in what appeared to be the desert. I didn't drown in what appeared to be a tsunami. I didn't sink in what appeared to be quick sand. I was in the valley, growing and developing in extreme temperatures and as my roots deepened they became stronger. After that season was over, I had matured, my thick leaves had finally unfolded, and out I popped! Once my bloom unfurled, the sweet fragrance of endurance, perseverance, and faith in God wafted through the air. Then the crescendo of this life event sounded as the Lord hand-plucked and placed me in a beautiful crystal vase that reflects the light of His glory. Now, as His center piece I am on display to assist in restoring the broken-hearted.

Once my bloom unfurled, the sweet fragrance of endurance, perseverance, and faith in God wafted through the air.

You are strong, valuable and great. You have so much to offer humanity. Trust God like you've never trusted Him before. Wrap your roots around others and strengthen someone. There is a new day dawning! Your green leaves are unfolding! You're just about to blossom!

Never, ever forget from whence the Lord has brought you. Go through the process of crushing, breaking, falling, getting back up again even if it is in a state of perplexity and distress. Never forget your journey. Never forget that your life is not over, only altered!

Until we meet again...

Growing is painful isn't it?
Write about your "lily" experience.

Now that you have come to the end of my journey, write about the beginning of your new journey.

About the Author

Debra D. Winans is CEO of Vertical Principle, Inc. and President of Point of Contact Concierge Service. Both companies were designed to catapult businesses and individuals into their next dimension of success and profitability.

With more than two decades of experience helping build leading organizations (both religious and secular), Debra has an uncanny ability to refine business operations and reconnect them to their original mission and goals, in order to drive the company's production capacity and profitability. Ms. Winans brilliantly identifies the crucial areas that need to be reconstructed to revitalize the leadership and to promote vitality and growth in deprived areas.

Many can attest to Debra's effectiveness including Agape Christian Fellowship in Arlington, Texas, where she served as the Business Operations Administrator. This is where Debra admits, "My passion grew to another dimension of excellence. It helped me to develop a wholesome view of corporate and biblical principles of leadership and servant hood."

But Debra became acquainted with servant hood in its purest form working with Mercy Ministries of America, Inc., where she served as Program Director, Counselor, and Public Relations Director. During her tenure, she had the privilege of reaching and mentoring emotionally damaged girls. In that season, Ms. Winans learned the principle of success that she now shares with visionaries and leaders all across America. Debra serves as president of The Shopping Bag of Bethlehem Centers of Nashville.

Debra's undying faith and belief that all things work out for your good, has led her to provide support and direction to many highly respected individuals and organizations. But it is her passion for motivating people to operate in a Spirit of Excellence that has moved her into international circles; providing her the opportunity to serve as Regional Director for the CEO Network in Nassau, Bahamas. CEO's and celebrities alike have called on Debra's skills and insight to coach and train their staff in service and hospitality.

Debra's gift for training and equipping individuals for the joy of serving their authorities is also being utilized to train armor bearers and leaders for Celebration of Life Church in Hendersonville, Tennessee where she faithfully serves under Pastors Joseph and Yolanda Morgan.

Ms. Winans has earned numerous certificates for teaching, training and counseling. It is no wonder that she has become a highly sought motivational speaker and teacher, gracing colleges and conferences all over the country. Her pearls of wisdom, foresight and understanding are precious commodities that many are seeking.

Write me, I would love to hear about your journey.
www.debradwinans.com

Made in the USA
Columbia, SC
30 June 2021

41212711R00076